HP LOVECRAFT

HP LOVECRAFT

THE MYSTERIOUS MAN BEHIND THE DARKNESS

CHARLOTTE MONTAGUE

CHARTWELL
BOOKS

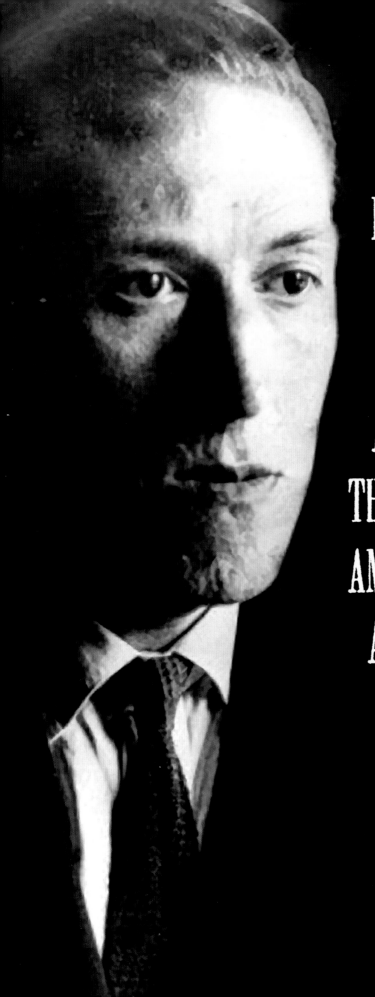

I KNOW ALWAYS THAT I AM AN OUTSIDER; A STRANGER IN THIS CENTURY AND AMONG THOSE WHO ARE STILL MEN.

H.P. LOVECRAFT
THE OUTSIDER

CONTENTS

INTRODUCTION

'Life is a hideous thing, and from the background behind what we know of it peer daemoniacal hints of truth which make it sometimes a thousandfold more hideous.'

How does one begin to explain the phenomenon that is H.P. Lovecraft? On first glance, he could be viewed as fairly repulsive. After all, he was decidedly racist, vehemently reactionary and viewed all 'direct erotic manifestations' as repellent. He was frustratingly uncommercial, disdainful of democracy and resolutely against technological progress. He viewed humanity as if from a distance, believing it to be nothing within the great scheme of things – one day it would disappear along with everything else.

However, this misanthropic visionary also displayed extraordinary kindness to those who knew him and corresponded with him

– and what a diligent correspondent he was, believed to have written around 100,000 letters in his lifetime. He nurtured their talent – gently tutoring, not teaching – in the process enhancing the careers of some fine writers. His generosity was astonishing, sharing his work and revising the work of others, sometimes writing the entire text of a story and taking no credit.

Above all, of course, there is his writing and its impact upon readers. French writer and Lovecraft fan Michel Houellebecq has described his reaction to first discovering Lovecraft: 'I myself discovered HPL at 16 through the intermediary of a "friend". To

The shadow man – H.P. Lovecraft, 1930.

call it a shock would be an understatement. I had not known literature was capable of this. And, what's more, I'm still not sure it is. There is something not really literary about Lovecraft's work.'

Appreciating the Great Texts

Lovecraft wrote many stories, but, between 1926 and 1934 he produced a series of masterly tales that are known to scholars as the 'great texts'. These are 'The Call of Cthulhu' (1926); 'The Color Out of Space' (1927); 'The Dunwich Horror' (1928); 'The Whisperer in Darkness' (1930); *At the Mountains of Madness* (1931); 'The Dreams in the Witch House' (1932); *The Shadow Over Innsmouth* (1932); and *The Shadow Out of Time* (1934).

These marvelous tales show Lovecraft at the top of his game. The language is honed to perfection, the atmosphere of increasing doom and hopelessness in the face of the universe is palpable and his complex mythology is ever-present, ready to awaken and regain its rightful position on earth when the stars align.

Nowadays, H.P. Lovecraft and the universe he created are part of an astonishing cultural phenomenon. Having died virtually unknown except to a small coterie of friends and associates, Lovecraft's reputation has been revived to the point that he is now revered. His work has been freshly appraised and he occupies a position of great respect within American literature. If evidence were needed, the fact that his work has been published in three annotated editions by Penguin Classics, or that respected French author and thinker, Michel Houellebecq, has written a biographical essay about him – *H.P. Lovecraft: Against the World, Against Life* – should go some way to confirming it. At last Lovecraft's achievement is being understood and his writing is being treated seriously.

Future Horror

His macabre work, circulated in his lifetime only in amateur periodicals and pulp magazines, can now be found in a wide variety of media. It seems tailor-made for the modern-day computer age and is beloved of heavy metal musicians. There are role-playing games, interactive computer games and many films, all of which generate monstrous new ways that Cthulhu, Lovecraft's signature octopus monster, can stalk your house and take over your life.

To understand how Lovecraft became the master of the horror genre, it is necessary to understand his life in his beloved Providence, to examine the way this fugitive from the eighteenth century lived and to meet the characters with whom he exchanged thousands of letters during his life. In that way, perhaps, we can begin to understand the man behind the darkness.

Portrait of the author – H.P. Lovecraft, 1921.

PART I
SHADOW MAN
OUT OF TIME

CHAPTER 1

THE GOLDEN CHILD

The Prosperous Side of Providence

At 9.00 a.m. on August 20, 1890, Howard Phillips Lovecraft came into the world, at 194 (to be re-numbered 454 in 1895 – 96) Angell Street on the prosperous eastern side of Providence. His parents, Winfield (1853 – 98) and Susie Phillips (1857 – 1921), had been married for just a year but would soon move out to rented accommodation in the south Boston suburb of Dorchester.

Married life looked set to be something of a disappointment for the highly strung Susie. Her husband, a lowly traveling salesman, was well below the social status to which she was accustomed and was unlikely to be able to provide her with the lifestyle she had enjoyed growing up.

It was probably for this reason that the union was not entirely to the liking of Susie's family. This may explain the fact that their marriage took place at an Episcopalian church in Boston rather than in Providence where there were a number of churches of that denomination in which they could easily have been married.

Winfield Lovecraft

Lovecraft's father, Winfield Lovecraft, was born on October 26, 1853 and named after United States General Winfield Scott who had made an unsuccessful bid for the presidency the previous year. Winfield's father, George, was a harness maker who lived for most of his life in Rochester, Massachusetts.

Married to Helen Allgood, George Lovecraft was father to five children, two of whom died in infancy. Winfield's surviving siblings were Emma Jane (1847 – 1925) and Mary Louise (1855 – 1916). Winfield married Sarah Susan Phillips – known as 'Susie' – on June 12, 1889 and they had one child –

Howard Phillips Lovecraft. Susie Lovecraft would become the central figure in H.P. Lovecraft's life.

In 1870, George Lovecraft moved his family to New York City but Winfield did not go with them. By this time, he was employed as a blacksmith for James Cunningham & Son, a carriage-making firm and was boarding with his uncle, John Full Lovecraft on Marshall Street.

Little is known about Winfield after that and although H.P. Lovecraft suggested that his father attended military school – 'in youth [he] gave up an appointment to West Point only to please his mother' – no trace of his attendance at any military establishment has been found. He finally moved to New York City which was the place of residence listed on his marriage certificate. He was employed by the large company of Gorham & Co., Silversmiths. It is not known how Winfield and Sarah Susan Phillips met but when they married, she was 31 and he was four years older.

Sarah, Howard and Winfield Lovecraft, 1892.

MATERNAL ANTECEDENTS

The results of Lovecraft's investigations into his maternal ancestry have proved to be every bit as dubious as those of his father's side. He wrote in 1915 that the first Phillips of his line arrived in western Rhode Island from Lincolnshire, England, in the late seventeenth century and the Phillips family could indeed trace its lineage in America back to the Massachusetts Bay Colony that was founded in 1630.

Nine years later, he was claiming that he was descended from the Reverend George Phillips (d. 1644) who had left England in 1630 and had settled in Watertown, Massachusetts, a town located just a few miles west of Cambridge. Lovecraft claimed – probably erroneously – that George was the father of Michael Phillips (1630? – 86?) who lived in Newport, Rhode Island and was definitely an ancestor of Lovecraft.

Michael's great-grandson, Asaph Phillips (1764 – 1829) settled around 1788 in Foster, Rhode Island and married Esther Whipple with whom he had eight children, all of whom survived childhood. Jeremiah Phillips, the sixth child, came to a tragic end. He died when his coat became tangled in machinery at a grist mill he owned in Foster, dragging him into the machine. His wife having died earlier the same year, their children – Susan, James, Whipple and Abbie – were orphaned.

PATERNAL ANTECEDENTS

Although it can be traced back to the Norman Conquest, the Lovecraft name first appears in 1450, on heraldic charts locating the family near the River Teign on the east coast of the county of Devon in southwest England. The first direct ancestor of the line that ended with Howard Phillips Lovecraft emerged with a John Lovecraft in 1560.

It is little surprise that the ever-inquisitive writer himself carried out investigations into his family's past. As he put it, 'Well – *John* begat *Richard* who begat *William* who begat *George* who begat *Joseph* who begat *John* who begat *Thomas* who begat *Joseph* who begat *George* who begat *Winfield* who begat your antient Grandpa.'

However, Kenneth W. Faig Jr has attempted and failed to confirm the male names of the Lovecraft line prior to Joseph Lovecraft who lived from 1775 until 1850 who would have been the writer's great-grandfather. It is likely, in fact, that Lovecraft's descent was not from any of the more noble lines that he claimed. Indeed, a number of the family connections he claimed are widely disputed, including his assertion that he was related through his mother to John Field (1520 – 87), the 'proto-Copernican' English astronomer.

Of course, given Lovecraft's fascination with astronomy, this would have been of consummate interest to him as, in the 1550s and 1560s, Field published works that were the first in English to discuss the principles of Copernican theory. A John Field (d. 1686) was one of the first settlers to establish himself in Providence, Rhode Island – Lovecraft's hometown – and it was from him that Lovecraft was directly descended and it is debatable that he is connected with the sixteenth century astronomer of the same name.

It would have dismayed the writer who was particularly irritated by the number of clergymen in his paternal line of descent and by his ancestry in general – 'No philosophers – no artists – no writers – not a cursed soul I could possibly talk to without getting a pain in the neck,' he wrote. Nonetheless, he was inordinately proud of his English roots and was happy to boast of his English antecedents on both sides of his bloodline. Indeed, he was enamoured of the notion of Englishness and believed the American Revolution to have been a terrible mistake.

Whipple Phillips

Whipple Van Buren Phillips (1833 – 1904), Lovecraft's grandfather on his mother's side, would become a crucial influence on the writer's life when he was a child. Whipple worked briefly as a teacher in the Foster area and in 1856 married his first cousin, Robie Alzada Place (1827 – 96). Three months after the wedding, Lillian Delora (1856 – 1932), another important person in Lovecraft's life, was born and four others followed: Sarah Susan, Emeline (1859 – 65), Edwin Everett (1864 – 1918) and Annie Emeline (1866 – 1941). They all lived in a house built by Robie's father, Stephen Place.

Whipple owned and ran a general store from 1855 for a couple of years before using the profit he made when he sold the store to launch a career as an entrepreneur and land speculator. In Coffin's Corner, just south of Foster, he built a mill, cottages in which his employees could live and an assembly hall for the use of the community. He changed the town's name to Greene, in honour of the Revolutionary War hero, Nathanael Greene who was born in Warwick, Rhode Island. Whipple, who would earn and lose several fortunes in the course of his life, was the owner of a town at the age of just 24.

He made a brief foray into local politics, serving from 1870 until 1872 in the lower house of the Rhode Island state legislature but he experienced a serious financial setback which forced him to move his family to Providence, Rhode Island, around 1874. They finally settled at 276 Broadway, not far from his office at 5 Custom House Street near the Providence River. By this time, he was running a fringing machine business, manufacturing the fringes that decorated curtains, bedspreads and clothing at the time. In 1878, he traveled to Paris to visit the Universal Exposition and would visit Europe on many occasions on business. A man of substance once again, in 1881 he completed the construction of a house at 194 Angell Street.

Owyhee Land and Irrigation Company

Around this time, Whipple became involved in an ambitious scheme that would eventually be his undoing. The Owyhee Land and Irrigation Company in Owyhee County in southwest Idaho was established in order to undertake the damming of the Bruneau River, a tributary of the Snake River, so that irrigation could be provided for the area's farms and fruit growing businesses. Initially, when the company was incorporated as the Snake River Company in 1884, with Whipple as president and his nephew Jeremiah, son of his brother James, as secretary and treasurer, it was advertised as dealing in land and livestock. Soon, however, Whipple was preoccupied with the idea of damming the river and, to reflect this, in 1889 the company name changed to the Owyhee Land and Irrigation Company.

The dam was built between 1887 and 1890 at a cost of $70,000 and near it Whipple created another town, naming it Grand View. By 1890, more than three hundred people lived there. Disaster struck on March 5, 1890, however, when the dam burst after being badly damaged by high waters. Whipple was not to be beaten, though, and by February 1893 he had completed another dam.

Whipple Phillips, Lovecraft's grandfather.

Around 1900, the Owyhee Land and Irrigation Company seems to have undergone some financial difficulties and in 1901 it was sold to five purchasers – one of whom was Whipple Phillips – at a sheriff's sale in Silver City. By this time it was valued at only $9,430. The final nail in the coffin came four years later when once again the dam was destroyed by heavy waters. It was a disaster not just for Whipple Phillips but also for Lovecraft's entire family. Just a few months later, Whipple died, aged 70, of a stroke probably brought on by stress.

A Damned Futile Business

His grandfather's death had a devastating impact on Lovecraft on whose intellectual development Whipple had a great influence. For a start, the family fortune had dwindled, Whipple's estate being valued at only $25,000. Of that, Susie inherited $5,000 and Lovecraft $2,500. Furthermore, the move from the house in which he had been brought up devastated the 14 year-old Lovecraft and even made him contemplate suicide:

> 'How could an old man of 14 (& I surely felt that way!) readjust his existence to a skimpy flat & new household programme & inferior outdoor setting in which almost nothing familiar remained. It seemed like a damned futile business to keep on living ... Oh Hell! Why not slough off consciousness altogether!'

He resisted the urge, he said, because there was still too much to learn about the world – 'certain elements – notably scientific curiosity & a sense of world drama held me back' – and, anyway, he could not make his mind up on the best method.

Susie Phillips

Susie Phillips was born on October 17, 1857 in her parents' first home in Foster. Like her sister, Lillian, she attended the Wheaton Female Seminary from at least 1871 – 72 but little more is known of her until her marriage. A friend of the Lovecraft family, Clara Hess, described her as 'very pretty and attractive, with a beautiful and unusually white complexion – got, it is said, by eating arsenic, although whether there is any truth to this story I do not know. She was an intensely nervous person.' It has been speculated that the arsenic she consumed in order to preserve a porcelain complexion might have contributed to her later physical and mental health issues. Clara Hess further described her as having 'a peculiarly shaped nose which rather fascinated me, as it gave her a very enquiring expression. Howard looked very much like her.'

As a mother, Susie would become a dominant force in Lovecraft's life, but she fretted about him almost from birth. Her friend, Ella Sweeney, recalls that during a holiday Susie had with her son in Dudley, Massachusetts, Lovecraft's mother was unable to stay still downstairs when her young son was asleep upstairs. When Miss Sweeney took the boy for a walk, Susie instructed her to stoop down when she was holding his hand, for fear, she claimed, that Howard's shoulder would be dislocated. This may have contributed to the hypochondria exhibited by Lovecraft, especially during his childhood, a malaise that would prevent him attending school for many years.

Louise Imogen Guiney

In 1892, with finances tight, the Lovecraft family moved to another Boston suburb, Auburndale, to the west of the city, where they lodged in the house of the well-known poet Louise Imogen Guiney (1861 – 1920). Meanwhile, they were planning to have a house built outside of Boston, a plan that, unfortunately, was never realized. Miss Guiney lived with her mother and several servants and worked at various jobs, bolstering her income with the rent the Lovecrafts paid. It was little more than a means to an end for her, as can be seen from several letters she wrote during the spring and summer of 1892:

Little Sunshine –
Lovecraft, aged 2.

*'Two confounded heathen are coming to
BOARD this summer.'* [30 *May*] *'There
are two and a half of them, as I said
atrocious Philistines whom I hate with
enthusiasm.'* [14 *June*] *'The unmentionables
are gone and we are our own mistresses
again.'* [30 *July*]

Nonetheless, Lovecraft spoke fondly of
Miss Guiney and especially of her dogs, large
St Bernards that were named after great
literary figures. His favorite was Brontë who
would lope along beside his baby carriage as
his mother pushed him along the street. As
was customary at the time, Howard's hair
was allowed to grow long and was styled in
long, golden ringlets, leading Miss Guiney's
mother to dub him 'Little Sunshine'.

Meanwhile, the poet made the precocious
baby Howard learn verses of poetry and
recite them in front of her visiting friends.
She taught him to answer her question
'Whom do you love?' with 'Louise Imogen
Guiney!' It was perhaps around this time that
Lovecraft showed the first inkling of interest
in literature and especially poetry. He later
wrote:

*'At the age of two I was a rapid talker,
familiar with the alphabet from my blocks
& picture books & ... absolutely meter-mad!
I could not read but would repeat any poem
of simple sort with unfaltering cadence ... not
that my rendition was necessarily notable,
but because my age lent uniqueness to the
performance.'*

Guiney did, indeed, become fairly
renowned as a poet. After her death in 1920,
at least two books about her were published
and Lovecraft was always proud of the fact
that his family had been associated with
her. The illustrious author Oliver Wendell
Holmes, a regular visitor to the Guiney
household, predicted great things for her and
her writing. He is also said to have sat the
young Lovecraft on his knee.

Winfield's Psychosis

From 1890 to 1893, Winfield Lovecraft's
work as a commercial traveler kept him away
from home a great deal and Lovecraft later
said 'my image of him is but vague.' In reality,
he was only in his son's life for the first two
and a half years of his life and even then his
business trips often meant he was gone for
long periods.

In April 1893, Lovecraft's life was
irrevocably changed when his father fell ill
while visiting Chicago on business. He was
admitted to Providence's Butler Hospital
– an insane asylum – for treatment and the
hospital records give an indication of how
serious his collapse was:

*'For a year past he has shown obscure
symptoms of mental disease – doing and
saying strange things at times; has also grown
pale and thin in flesh. He continued his
business, however, until Apr. 21, when he
broke down completely while stopping in
Chicago. He rushed from his room shouting
that a chambermaid had insulted him, and
that certain men were outraging his wife in*

the room above [Susie was not in Chicago at the time]. *He was extremely noisy and violent for two days, but was finally quieted by free use of the bromides, which made his removal here possible.'*

Winfield would remain in Butler Hospital for five years until his death on July 19, 1898 and in all that time Lovecraft was never taken to visit his father. The illness that eventually killed him has always been a mystery. On his death certificate, the cause of death is listed as 'general paresis' and Lovecraft claimed that Winfield died of a paralyzing stroke that had sent him into a coma from which he never woke up.

Medical advances since then, however, suggest that Winfield's psychosis was probably caused by syphilis and his behavior when he was admitted to the hospital certainly displays a number of the symptoms of tertiary syphilis, including paranoia and delusions. During his time in hospital, he became violent, claimed that his food was being poisoned. His lifestyle as a traveling salesman opens up the possibility of his having contracted syphilis from a prostitute during one of his stopovers, but, given that it can take many years for the extreme symptoms to occur, it is more probable that he contracted the disease before his marriage.

Back to Angell Street

With the onset of Winfield's illness in 1893, Susie and Howard immediately moved back to Angell Street and the comfort of the Phillips family. They had little choice because, as Winfield had not earned much, they had little in the way of savings to fall back upon. And, of course, being a member of the illustrious Phillips family it was inconceivable that she would go out and work to support her and her son.

Howard's world would never be the same again. For a start, from now onwards he would be even more under the influence of women, especially the smothering attention of Susie, but also his two aunts, Lillian and Annie, his grandmother Robie and the maidservants. It was his mother's influence that dominated, however.

Still, the move to Angell Street was far from a bad thing. Lovecraft had lost his father, or, at least would never see him again, but he now entered a comfortable and happy stage of his life where he enjoyed the security of Phillips family life but was also given complete freedom to pursue the intellectual interests that would define his life.

He had all the means to do so because shortly after Winfield was admitted to hospital, Howard's grandfather sent him the entire Lovecraft family library. Furthermore, the house on Angell Street was filled with opportunities for a young boy. It had fifteen rooms on three stories, with the four servants living in the attic. The large garden had an orchard, a fountain and numerous trees and there was also a carriage house where the horses were stabled and the family's carriage was kept. Above this were the living quarters of the coachman.

My Beloved Grandfather

Also contributing to the good life upon which the young Lovecraft was embarking was the beneficial presence of his doting maternal grandfather, Whipple Phillips. '... my beloved grandfather ... became the center of my entire universe,' he later wrote, confirming his love and respect. Whipple's contribution to the intellectual development of H.P. Lovecraft cannot be overestimated and he cured him of his fear of the dark, an ironic notion given the stories he would pen in later life. When the boy was 5 years old, Whipple dared him to walk through some of the dark rooms in the Angell Street house. Mostly, however, he showed him *objets d'art* that he had brought back from Europe, wrote letters to him when he was away on his frequent business trips and, best of all, made up weird tales that he recited to the terrified boy.

They were good times. Whipple's business interests were flourishing and his finances were in good order. Lovecraft began around this time to pay attention to his surroundings and, in particular, the town in which he lived:

> *'I was born in the year 1890 in a small town, & in a section of that town which during my childhood lay not more than four blocks (N. & E.) from the actual primal & open New England countryside, with rolling meadows, stone walls, cart paths, brooks, deep woods, mystic ravines, lofty river bluffs, planted fields, white antient farmhouses, barns & byres, gnarled hillside orchards, great lone elms, & all the authentick marks of a rural milieu unchanged since the 17th & 18th centuries ... My house, tho' an urban one on a paved street, had spacious grounds & stood next to an open field with a stone wall ... where great elms grew & my grandfather had corn & potatoes planted, & a cow pastured under the gardener's care.'*

A Strange Magic

Already, though, his vivid imagination was beginning to turn his surroundings into the places of dread that would haunt his writing in years to come:

> *'When I was three years old I felt a strange magic & fascination (not unmixed with a vague unease & perhaps a touch of mild fear) in the ancient houses of Providence's venerable hill ... with their fanlighted doorways, railed flights of steps, & stretches of brick sidewalk.'*

At the age of 6, Lovecraft rebelled against the golden ringlets and girlish clothing his mother had made him wear and she wept bitter tears as his locks were shorn. Before that, grandfather Whipple had tried to persuade Lovecraft to dress like a little boy. In a letter from June 1894, he wrote, 'I will tell you more about what I have seen when I get home if you are a good boy and wear trousers.'

But still Susie would spoil her son, refusing to let him out of her sight, and walking alongside him to ensure that he did not fall off whenever he went out on his tricycle. He was hugely indulged, being given whatever he wanted. 'My array of toys, books, and other youthful pleasures was virtually unlimited,' he wrote.

A Precocious Child

Cocooned though he was in a physical sense, he was by no means isolated intellectually. Even in play, he had begun to create fantastic worlds. There was a vacant piece of ground next to the house in Angell Street in which the family's coachman built a playhouse in 1894 – 95 that the boy named the 'Engine House'. He created a toy railway system that ran between this area and the house and built a steam engine for the railway, 'a sort of queer boiler on a tiny express-wagon'.

The coachman lived with his wife in the rooms above the stable, but when Whipple Phillips was forced to let him go in 1900 as money got tighter, Lovecraft turned the space into his private play area, extending the railway into it. A little later Lovecraft enlisted the help of some local children to build a little fortified Alaskan village in the area beside the house. He called it New Anvik, a name he borrowed from Kirk Munroe's children's book *Snow Shoes and Sledges*.

These imaginary worlds remained Lovecraft's escape for many years and even when he and his mother were forced by Whipple's death to relocate to a smaller Angell Street property in 1904, Lovecraft recreated New Anvik in another empty space beside his new home. In fact, he would continue to play in this area until the comparatively late age of 17 when he realized at last that he was probably too old to be playing with toys. 'Big boys do not play in toy houses and mock gardens,' he wrote, 'so I was obliged to turn over my world in sorrow to another and younger boy who dwelt across the lot from me.'

A Gateway to Glittering Vistas

As we have seen, Lovecraft was capable of learning poetry at an early age and reciting it confidently and precociously to the adults with whom he was surrounded. Having learned the alphabet at the age of two, Lovecraft claimed that he began to read with ease at the age of 4, *Grimm's Fairy Tales* being one of the earliest books he enjoyed. These fairy tales he later wrote 'were my truly representative diet, & I lived mostly in a medieval world of imagination.' At the age of 5, he discovered a book that was to become pivotal in the development of his creativity and his intellect – the *Arabian Nights*. Lovecraft said of it:

'... how many dream-Arabs have the Arabian Nights bred! I ought to know, since at the age of 5 I was one of them! I ... found in Lang's Arabian Nights a gateway to glittering vistas of wonder and freedom. It was then that I invented for myself the name of Abdul Alhazred, and made my mother take me to the Oriental curio shops and fit me up an Arabian corner in my room.'

The *Arabian Nights* became the first of a series of obsessions that gripped Lovecraft's imagination throughout his childhood and teenage years. He adopted the persona of Abdul Alhazred (a play on the words *all has read*) and dressed as an Arab. The name Abdul Alhazred would become important to the Cthulhu Mythos as the 'Mad Arab' who was the supposed author of his fictional grimoire – the *Necronomicon*. Lovecraft was unclear exactly how he came upon this name. In his autobiographical essay, *Notes on a Nonentity*, he says that Abdul Alhazred had come about after 'some kindly elder had suggested [it] to me as a typical Saracen name.'

The Rime of the Ancient Mariner

The *Arabian Nights* may not have made a huge contribution to Lovecraft's interest in weird fiction, but his discovery at the age of 6 of Samuel Taylor Coleridge's poem, *The Rime of the Ancient Mariner* played a bigger role in steering him in the direction of the weird. Illustrated by Gustave Doré, it made a great and lasting impression upon him:

'Imagine a tall, stately Victorian library in a house sometimes visited with my mother or aunts. Marble mantel – thick bearskin rug – endless shelves of books ... a house of adults, so that a 6 year-old caller's interest strays most naturally to the shelves & great center table & mantel. Fancy then the discovery of a great atlas-sized gift-book leaning against the mantel & having on the cover gilt letters reading 'With illustrations by Gustave Doré'.

The Mariner (1866) from *The Rime of the Ancient Mariner*, illustrated by Gustave Doré.

LUCIFER, KING OF HELL
BY GUSTAVE DORÉ (1832 – 1883)

One of the most popular and successful artists of his day, Doré drew this illustration of Lucifer for Canto XXXIV of Dante's *Divine Comedy: Inferno* between 1861 and 1868. Lovecraft wrote in a 1916 letter to Rheinhart Kleiner that Doré's illustrations were the possible source of his 'night-gaunts' – dreams and nightmares that would eventually inspire his writing.

The title didn't matter – for didn't I know the dark, supernatural magic of the Doré pictures in our Dante & Milton at home? I open the book – & behold a hellish picture of a corpse-ship with ragged sails under a waning moon! I turn a page ... God! a spectral, half-transparent ship on whose deck a corpse & a skeleton play at dice! By this time I am flat on the bearskin rug & ready to thumb through the whole book ... of which I've never heard before ... A sea full of rotting serpents & death-fires dancing in the black air ... troops of angels & daemons ... crazed, dying, distorted forms ... dead men rising in their putrescence & lifelessly manning the dark rigging of a fate-doomed barque ...'

The Night-Gaunts Begin

The death, in 1895, of his paternal grandfather does not seem to have affected young Howard a great deal as he had never met him in person but the loss the following January of his maternal grandmother, Robie Phillips did impact upon his life:

'The death of my grandmother plunged the household into a gloom from which it never fully recovered. The black attire of my mother & aunts terrified & repelled me to such an extent that I would surreptitiously pin bits of bright cloth or paper to their skirts for sheer relief.'

The cloud that hung over the Angell Street house had a serious effect on the five-and-a-half year-old boy. He began to suffer from terrifying nightmares featuring creatures that he dubbed 'night-gaunts' and which he suspected might derive from Doré's illustrations in an edition of *Paradise Lost* that he stumbled upon in the house's east parlour. He described them later as 'black, lean, rubbery things with bared, barbed tails, bat-wings, and *no faces at all.*'

The house at 454 Angell Street, Providence, *c.* 1895

He struggled each night to remain awake so that he might not be visited by these horrific creatures and he was still fearful of them fifteen years later. Of course, terrifying though these dreams may have been, they would, in the fullness of time, provide inspiration and imagery for a number of his mature tales, especially in elements such as the helplessness of a victim confronted with beings and forces far more powerful than himself. These horror tales lay thirty years in the future but they were undoubtedly colored by his nightmares on Angell Street.

New Passions Grow

Around this time, Lovecraft developed his lifelong love for the eighteenth century, a love that grew during the long hours he spent leafing through the books in the house's windowless attic. His fascination with the period is evident in a later description of a trip to Western Rhode Island.

> *In* 1896 ... [*I*] *met an ancient gentlewoman – a Mrs Wood ... who was celebrating her hundredth birthday. Mrs Wood was born in* 1796, *and could walk and talk when Genl. Washington breath'd his last. And now, in* 1896, *I was conversing with her – with one who had talked to people in periwigs and three-cornered hats, and had studied from schoolbooks with the long s! Young as I was, the idea gave me a tremendous feeling of cosmic victory over Time.'*

As Lovecraft himself said, 'I think I am probably the only living person for whom the 18th century idiom is actually a prose & poetic mother tongue.' He explained how the downstairs rooms of the house were filled with standard nineteenth-century Victorian furniture and fittings, while the attic with its 'crumbling and long-s'd tomes of every size and nature – *Spectator, Tatler, Guardian, Idler, Rambler*, Dryden, Pope, Thomson, Young, Tickell, Cooke's *Hesiod*, Ovid by various hands, Francis's Horace and Phaedrus, &c. &c. &c ...' took him back in time to the period in which he longed to live.

The subject matter of much of the eighteenth-century literature that Lovecraft read came from classical antiquity and this became the boy's next obsession. Now aged 6, he read Nathaniel Hawthorne's *A Wonderbook for Girls and Boys* and *Tanglewood Tales*, in which Hawthorne retold classical myths for children. Thomas Bulfinch's *The Age of Fable, or Stories of Gods and Heroes*, was another simplified retelling of the myths of antiquity that captivated Lovecraft and brought his *Arabian Nights* phase to an end.

He also had the souvenirs that Whipple Phillips had brought back with him from his visits to Rome – mosaics, paintings and other *objets d'art*. Roman coins that Whipple brought back to Providence thrilled the boy with the thought that they had been created by actual Roman engravers and mints, but had also passed through the hands of real Roman citizens two thousand years previously.

A Confession of Unfaith

He became a regular at the Rhode Island School of Design in Providence that he described as 'a true magick grotto where unfolded before me the glory that was Greece and the grandeur that was Rome'. He visited museums of classical antiquity such as the Museum of Fine Arts and the Fogg Museum at Harvard, started to collect plaster reproductions of the Greek and Roman gods and goddesses, taught himself the Greek alphabet and began to learn the intricacies of Latin grammar. Abdul Alhazred was banished and replaced with Lucius Valerius Messala. He even had a religious epiphany of sorts that he described in 'A Confession of Unfaith':

> *When about seven or eight I was a genuine pagan, so intoxicated with the beauty of Greece that I acquired a half-sincere belief in the old gods and nature-spirits. I have in literal truth built altars to Pan, Apollo, Diana and Athena, and have watched for dryads and satyrs in the woods*

and fields at dusk. Once I firmly thought I beheld some of these sylvan creatures dancing under autumnal oaks; a kind of "religious experience" as true in its way as the subjective ecstasies of any Christian. If a Christian tell me that he felt the reality of his Jesus or Javeh, I can reply that I have seen the hoofed Pan and the sisters of the Hespeian Phaëthusa.'

It was around this time that Lovecraft began to write, composing poetry recounting the exploits of gods and goddesses and short prose pieces. The first extant piece of work by him is dated November 8, 1897 – the 'second edition' of 'The Poem of Ulysses; or The Odyssey: Written for Young People'. It comes in the form of a little hand-made book to which he added a preface, a copyright notice and an internal title page that bore the legend:

THE YOUNG FOLKS' ULYSSES

OR THE ODYSSEY IN PLAIN OLDEN ENGLISH VERSE AN EPICK POEM WRIT BY HOWARD LOVECRAFT, GENT.

The work consisted of 88 lines of rhyming verse telling the story of Homer's *Odyssey*, albeit in a very simplified way, given that the original consisted of 12,000 lines. Nonetheless, just to have read Homer's *Odyssey* at the age of 7 was impressive.

The Providence Press Co.

Lovecraft had, without doubt, decided on a career as a writer because in the book he lists other books, both already written and still to come. Charmingly, after the preface is a 'P.S.' that promises 'The later works may be much better than this because the author will have more practice.' These works were probably sold to members of his family and as he had not yet become the owner of a means of printing, he would have had to write out each copy he sold.

Other books he lists in his 'Providence Classics' series for 'Providence Press Co.', as he calls his little publishing venture are: *Mythology for the Young*, 25 cents; *An Old Egyptian Myth Prepared Specially for Small Children*, 5 cents; 'soon to be published' *The Young Folks Iliad in Verse*, 5 cents; *The Aeneid*, 5 cents; and *Ovid's Metamorphoses*, 25 cents. The first two, it seems, were already written, but no copies have survived.

Being L. Valerius Messala

He embraced the religion of classical antiquity but was dismissive of the religion of Christians. Told at the age of 5 that Santa Claus was no more than a myth, he immediately asked why God was not a myth as well. Later, his skepticism about religion rendered him unwelcome at the Sunday school to which he was sent. His views were, indeed, strong in this area. 'I felt that one good Roman pagan was worth any six dozen of the cringing scum riffraff who took up with a fanatical foreign belief, and was frankly sorry that the Syrian superstition was not stamped out.' In another letter, Lovecraft noted that 'at seven I sported the adopted name of L. VALERIUS MESSALA & tortured imaginary Christians in amphitheatres'.

Lovecraft had now moved through several obsessions in his thus-far short life. He had devoured the *Arabian Nights* and had donned the guise of the 'Mad Arab', Abdul Alhazred, had embraced the mores and literature of the eighteenth century (an obsession that he would never quite leave behind) and had enjoyed the myths and legends of classical antiquity, disguised as Lucius Valerius Messala. His next fascination would color the remainder of his life and direct him towards the kind of writing for which he is so well remembered.

CHAPTER 2

SCIENCE & THE WEIRD

Discovering Edgar Allan Poe

In 1898, Lovecraft discovered the writing of Edgar Allan Poe. A master of mystery and the macabre, Poe himself died mysteriously in 1849. He was one of the first American short story writers and is often said to have invented the genre of detective fiction.

For H.P. Lovecraft, however, he was the greatest horror story writer who had ever put pen to paper. 'To him we owe the modern horror story in its final and perfected state,' he wrote in his essay 'Supernatural Horror in Literature'. Lovecraft even imitated his style occasionally in his work. He admits as much himself: 'Since Poe affected me most of all horror-writers, I can never feel that a tale starts out right unless it has something of his manner. I could never plunge into things abruptly, as the popular writers do. To my mind it is necessary to establish a setting and avenue of approach before the main show can adequately begin.'

Lovecraft particularly admired Poe's impartiality in the narration of his tales, saying he:

'... perceived the essential impersonality of the real artist; and knew that the function of creative fiction is merely to express and interpret events and sensations as they are, regardless of how they tend or what they prove – good or evil, attractive or repulsive, stimulating or depressing, with the author always acting as a vivid and detached chronicler rather than as a teacher, sympathizer, or vendor of opinion.'

The Night-Gaunts

But Lovecraft's liking for the type of strange stories of the sort that would come to be known as weird fiction did not derive from his encountering Edgar Allan Poe alone.

Grandpa Whipple also had a penchant for the weird and seeing that his grandson enjoyed it, made up stories that were drawn from the Gothic writings of late eighteenth century authors such as Horace Walpole, Matthew Gregory Lewis, Anne Radcliffe and others.

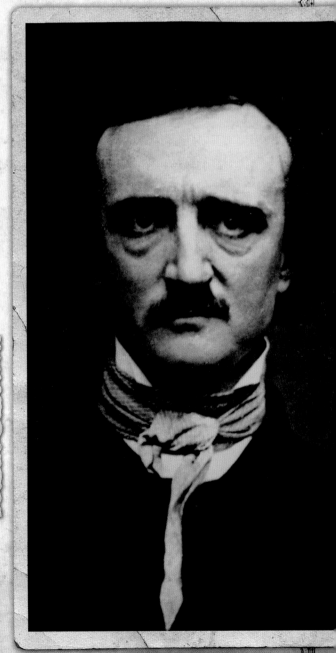

Master of Mystery – Edgar Allan Poe.

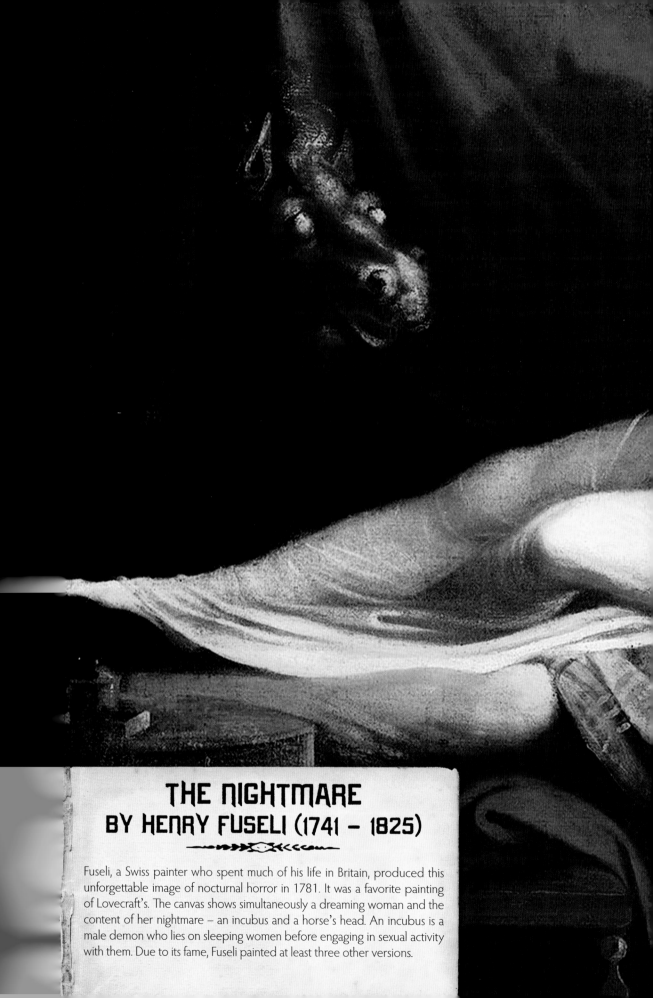

THE NIGHTMARE
BY HENRY FUSELI (1741 – 1825)

Fuseli, a Swiss painter who spent much of his life in Britain, produced this unforgettable image of nocturnal horror in 1781. It was a favorite painting of Lovecraft's. The canvas shows simultaneously a dreaming woman and the content of her nightmare – an incubus and a horse's head. An incubus is a male demon who lies on sleeping women before engaging in sexual activity with them. Due to its fame, Fuseli painted at least three other versions.

'I never heard oral weird tales except from my grandfather,' he later wrote in a letter, '... who, observing my tastes in reading, used to devise all sorts of impromptu original yarns about black woods, unfathomed caves, winged horrors (like the 'night-gaunts' of my dreams about which I used to tell him), old witches with sinister cauldrons, & deep, low moaning sounds. He drew most of his imagery from the early Gothic romances – Radcliffe, Lewis, Maturin, &c. – which he seemed to like better than Poe or other later fantaisistes.'

Pre-Poe Fiction

This led to Lovecraft's first piece of fiction writing – 'The Noble Eavesdropper' – a story that he dated to 1897. It did not survive and little is known about it apart from the fact that it concerned 'a boy who overheard some horrible conclave of subterranean beings in a cave.' However, he claimed that it was 'pre-Poe', before he had read the works of the master of mystery. Sources suggest that his other early stories showed little of the influence of Poe. These were 'The Little Glass Bottle', 'The Secret Cave; or John Lees Adventure', 'The Mystery of the Graveyard; or, A Dead Man's Revenge' and 'The Mysterious Ship'. Although not dated, it is likely that these stories were written between 1898 and 1902.

At the same time as he was discovering Poe, Lovecraft was studying violin and on one occasion performed a recital for family and friends. He studied from the age of 7 to 9 but music was not of great interest to him. He was also developing affection for the dime novels of the day, ironically, given his liking for the more highbrow end of literature. He voraciously devoured westerns, detective and espionage stories and tales of high school and college life.

Symptoms of Asperger's

1898 was a tumultuous year for Lovecraft. His father died, he discovered Poe and he began to take an interest in science. He also suffered what he later called a 'near-breakdown'. It is unclear what it involved because there is no medical record of it and he did not receive any treatment, but he suffered another two years later.

'I didn't inherit a very good set of nerves,' he later wrote, 'since near relatives on both sides of my ancestry were prone to headaches, nerve-exhaustion, and breakdowns.' In another letter, he described having a tendency towards chorea in childhood, his face being subject to 'unconscious & involuntary motions', facial tics that died down when he went to high school. The breakdown could have had something to do with the death of his father and the strain the last few years of his father's life had put on his mother.

Such frailty in a man with Lovecraft's physique was odd, however, for he was almost six feet tall, had broad shoulders and was well built. Nonetheless, he suffered from dreadful self-esteem, considering himself to be weak and an invalid. In fact, some sources suggest that nowadays a person like Lovecraft might be diagnosed to have Asperger's Syndrome, the symptoms of which include an inability to interact socially, a highly obsessive nature, emotional immaturity, anxiety and physical maladroitness. Sufferers are also reluctant to leave the environment with which they are familiar and this can certainly be said of Lovecraft who remained in Providence, apart from his brief sojourn in New York, much of his life.

A Sense of Pervading Doom

Two tales by Lovecraft's hand survive from the period 1903 – 08. 'The Beast in the Cave' and 'The Alchemist' do not betray his increasingly voracious reading of pulp magazines with their weird tales of horror, fantasy and science fiction, however. Edgar Allan Poe and the Gothics remain the predominant influences and the labored prose style reflects that of the eighteenth century Augustan essayists.

'The Beast in the Cave' is a story that

THE BEAST IN THE CAVE

'The Beast in the Cave' tells the story of a philosophy scholar who while visiting Mammoth Cave in Kentucky becomes separated from his guide. When his torch eventually gives out, he resigns himself to never finding the way out. When he suddenly hears strange non-human sounding footsteps approaching, he picks up a boulder and throws it in the direction of the sounds. The beast is struck by the stone and falls to the ground. Meanwhile, the guide finds the man and they examine the fallen beast using the guide's torchlight. As the creature breathes its last before them, they realize that it is a human who had, like the protagonist, become lost in the cave. Neither man is ever seen again.

THE ALCHEMIST

The narrator, Count Antoine de C- tells the tale of how, centuries ago, one of his ancestors had killed an evil wizard, Michel Mauvais. The wizard's son Charles placed a curse on all his descendants that they would die at the age of 32. The family suffers as a result until it is almost ruined financially and Count Antoine is the only one left. However, he is approaching 32. Exploring his castle, he finds a passage with a locked door at one end. As he starts to leave, he hears a noise and turns to see a figure standing in front of the door. The man attacks the count but is badly wounded by him. As he lies dying, he confesses that he is in fact Charles Mauvais, that he had discovered the elixir of eternal life and had personally fulfilled the curse for centuries.

externalizes Lovecraft's innate fear of darkness of which his grandfather had tried to cure him. It also launches his fascination in his writing with caves and tunnels. His style is deliberately archaic but we can see the beginning of his ability to create atmosphere and a sense of pervading doom. Lovecraft, always his own worst critic, described the story as 'ineffably pompous'.

Lovecraft imbues 'The Alchemist' with an extraordinary, medieval atmosphere. There are connections with Poe's themes, especially in the count's fascination with his own mental state and the fact that the protagonist has fallen on hard times. Lovecraft wrote other tales during these years, but all have been destroyed but these two.

Cover of an *Adventure Comics* adaptation of 'The Alchemist', 1992.

A Passion for Astronomy

The ever-inquisitive Lovecraft may have had an upbringing that was different to that of most boys of his time, but it did not prevent him having an interest in anatomy where it related to sex. Rather than wait to be told about the birds and the bees, he ploughed through the medical books in the family library. As he says, 'The result was the very opposite of what parents generally fear – for instead of giving me an abnormal & precocious interest in sex ... it virtually killed my interest in the subject.' Throughout his life, this last statement was borne out. He never had any romantic attachments as a youth and when he did eventually marry, it was only after three years of hard work and pursuit by the lady in question.

LOVECRAFT'S LOVE OF SCIENCE

If sex was not an obsession, science certainly was, or astronomy to be precise. It would become the third part of what Lovecraft described as his tripartite nature. The component of this were: love of the strange and fantastic, love of the ancient and permanent and love of abstract truth and scientific logic. He describes his love of science in 'A Confession of Unfaith':

'The most poignant sensations of my existence are those of 1896, when I discovered the Hellenic world, and of 1902, when I discovered the myriad suns and worlds of infinite space. Sometimes I think the latter event greater, for the grandeur of that growing conception of the universe still excites a thrill hardly to be duplicated. I made of astronomy my principal scientific study, obtaining larger and larger telescopes, collecting astronomical books to the number of sixty-one, and writing copiously on the subject in the form of special and monthly articles in the local daily press. By my thirteenth birthday I was thoroughly impressed with man's impermanence and insignificance, and by my seventeenth, about which time I did some particularly detailed writing on the subject, I had formed in all essential particulars my present pessimistic cosmic views. The futility of all existence began to impress and oppress me; and my references to human progress, formerly hopeful, began to decline in enthusiasm.'

The Sky at Night

A friend of the Phillips family, Professor John Howard Appleton, gave Lovecraft a copy of his beginner's guide to chemistry, *The Young Chemist*, and Lovecraft channeled his new passion into writing and publishing, launching the single-sheet *Scientific Gazette* on March 4, 1899. He also wrote several essays on chemistry that he sold for between 5 and 25 cents each. But by 1902 it was astronomy that was occupying his mind. Charles Augustus Young's *Lessons in Astronomy* was the first book on the subject he bought. Until then, he had been forced to rely on what he could find in the library in his attic room.

He had inherited some books from his maternal grandmother who had studied astronomy at the Smithville Seminary, a Baptist teachers' college in North Scituate, Rhode Island when younger. He was indulged in his new interest as usual. In the summer of 1903 his mother bought him a refractor telescope with a 2.25-inch objective lens. Through another friend of the family, Professor Winslow Upton, he was also fortunate enough to be allowed to use the 12-inch refractor telescope at Ladd Observatory at Brown University in Providence.

He was there, he said, every night that the sky was clear, pushing his bike up the hill to the observatory and then freewheeling back down in the middle of the night. In fact, he did so much observing that he suffered from

John Howard Appleton.

pain in his neck and it is said to have given him a stoop that led his mother, somewhat cruelly, to describe him as 'deformed'.

He began writing about astronomy, typing his pieces on an old Remington typewriter he bought in July 1906 and submitting them to local newspapers. He would continue to use this typewriter until his death. It was used to provide him with finished copy that he could send to publications but he always first wrote his pieces in longhand. Aged 15, he was contributing articles on astronomy to the *Pawtuxet Valley Gleaner* and wrote a column for the *Providence Tribune* that continued until he was 18.

An Expert Reputation

By 1909, Lovecraft had acquired a hectograph printing machine. The hectograph used a painstaking printing process that involved the transfer of a piece of text or an image created using special inks, onto a pan of gelatin or a gelatin pad that had been pulled tightly across a metal frame. He produced his publications in print runs of four copies. He was by now gaining a reputation as an expert astronomer and even gave a presentation of lantern-slides to family and invited guests at the Angell Street house. This was unusual as he disliked such gatherings. In fact, he would do anything to avoid even being engaged in conversation. Those who passed him in the street found that he would walk with his head down, reluctant to interact socially or to be taken out of his own world.

Astronomy appealed to Lovecraft as a career, but he failed to realize how vital it was that he be proficient in mathematics as astronomy relies on complex calculations. Unfortunately, in his brief time at high school he never excelled at algebra, writing that 'The first year I barely passed in algebra, but was so little satisfied with what I had accomplished, that I voluntarily repeated the last half of the term.'

Lovecraft the Recluse

On June 10, 1908, the 'Professor', as his classmates called him, left school without a diploma of any kind, having only studied as far as eleventh grade and entered the strangest period of his life, cutting himself off from the outside world for five years. He slept much of the day, seldom wore more than his bathrobe and ventured outside only at night when no one was around. It remains a mystery to this day what brought this period on, whether it was depression or another 'breakdown'.

'In 1908 I should have entered Brown University, but the broken state of my health rendered the idea absurd. I was and am a prey to intense headaches, insomnia, and general nervous weakness which prevents my continuous application to writing.'

It seems odd that Lovecraft believes his entry into university an inevitability when he never actually graduated from high school. Just how ill was he, though? At the time, it seems that his tics had by no means disappeared and descriptions of them sound more like seizures. Of course, we do not know if he withdrew from school purely because of them but they must have been a contributing factor.

One of his few boyhood friends, Harold W. Munro, puts the blame for his failing health and subsequent withdrawal from education on an undated fall Lovecraft had when he was exploring a building site. He fell from a ladder onto his head. Or was he just so devastated by his continued lack of success in algebra and the fact that it meant he would be unable to pursue a career in astronomy that he did not want to carry on.

Lovecraft wrote in 1931: 'That was the first major set-back I ever received – the first time I was ever brought up short against a consciousness of my own limitations. It was clear to me that I hadn't brains enough to be an astronomer – and that was a pill I couldn't swallow with equanimity.'

WEIRD FICTION

Weird fiction of the contemporary kind, disposed of the conventions of the nineteenth century Gothic tale and the ghost story and, rather, imbued the reader with a sense of creeping unease. The stories of writers such as Algernon Blackwood, Arthur Machen and Robert W. Chambers were not peopled with mythical monsters, vampires and werewolves. Instead, their protagonists were often doomed men for whom reality had become blurred. Often, they were scientists or explorers who were forced to undergo horrific physical transmutations or witness hideous rituals, the natural and scientific laws shattered in the process.

'My room became haunted with demons.'
Illustration by Mackay from 'The Woman's Ghost Story' by Algernon Blackwood, 1907.

The Wilderness Years

So, from 1908 until 1913 we have little idea what Lovecraft was doing. We know that he persevered with his scientific studies but found it difficult, often, he says, stopping because of excruciating headaches after only fifteen minutes. In 1910 he wrote 'A Brief Course in Inorganic Chemistry', of which no manuscript survives. Meanwhile, Susie Lovecraft, his mother, was becoming increasingly unstable and the pair were becoming poorer.

She must have been frustrated by Howard's lack of a profession and his educational failure must have deepened this feeling. Lovecraft's uncle, Edwin E. Phillips, lost him and Susie money in 1911, probably through bad investments, rendering their economic plight even worse. It has been said that Susie lavished both her love and her hate on her son and one incident demonstrates this. Susie's friend, Clara Hess, went to visit her and described later how 'Mrs Lovecraft talked continuously of her unfortunate son who was so hideous that he hid from everyone and did not like to walk upon the streets where people could gaze at him.' Lovecraft considered his distinctive, long, jutting jaw to be something of a physical defect but he also suffered badly from ingrown hairs on his face that he had to pull out with tweezers, leaving angry red cuts.

Weird Fiction and Amateur Writing

Much of Lovecraft's time during his five-year hiatus was spent reading his beloved pulp magazines such as *The Argosy*, *Cavalier* and *All-Story Magazine* which he particularly enjoyed as it featured fantasy and horror stories. He first began to read *Black Cat* magazine in 1904 and that and *All-Story* were the first sources of contemporary weird material that he found.

His interest in the weird developed. 'In 1913,' he wrote, 'I had formed the reprehensible habit of picking up cheap magazines like *The Argosy* to divert my mind from the tedium of reality.' He was undoubtedly enthralled by the tales of horror, fantasy, mystery and science fiction that he found between the covers of these cheap publications. They were mainly published by Frank Munsey who used new high-speed printing presses and inexpensive pulp paper to produce affordable magazines, generally selling for 10 cents.

In September 1913, Lovecraft took up his pen to write to the letters column of *The Argosy* – 'The Log-Book' – to fiercely criticize love stories by an author named Fred Jackson that were frequently printed in the magazine. He stirred up a hornet's nest of protest amongst other readers of the magazine, including a response in the form of a humorous poem from a reader named John Russell. Not to be outdone, Lovecraft fashioned what he termed 'a 44-line satire in the manner of Pope's *Dunciad*' that appeared in the magazine in January 1914. This continued for about a year until the magazine called a halt to it.

Writing for the UAPA

That would have been the end of it, had the president of the United Amateur Press Association not been a reader of *The Argosy*. The UAPA was an organization made up of amateur writers who were encouraged to publish their own little magazines and distribute them amongst friends and family, somewhat in the manner of Lovecraft's amateurish publications as a child. They were also encouraged to let others in the organization publish their work. An annual fee subscription was required and there was a conference every July at which elections were held for the organization's offices – president, treasurer, editor of its magazine and so on.

Edward F. Daas invited Lovecraft to join the UAPA, an invitation eagerly accepted by him in April 1914 as he was doing little else. It was an important moment that would give some point to his life and that would mark something of a revival of his spirits as well as his writing career. 'With the advent of the United I obtained a new will to live;' he wrote

'... a renewed sense of existence as other than a superfluous weight; and found a sphere in which I could feel my efforts were not wholly futile.'

For Lovecraft the world of amateur publishing was ideal. The members communicated, in the main, by mail, removing his natural shyness of people and he loved the fact that members were not driven by earning money from their writing.

Lovecraft's official United Amateur Press Association photograph, 1915.

They wrote because they loved doing so. It indulged his notion of himself as an English gentleman who had no truck with the nasty commercial world.

He threw himself into it, his first prose contribution – 'A Task for Amateur Journalists' – being published in the *New Member* in January 1915 and soon, his own magazine, *The Conservative*, saw the light of day. It would run to thirteen issues of sizes varying from 4 to 28 pages. Soon, he was being elected to prestigious positions in the UAPA, first as chairman of the rather pompously titled Department of Public Criticism and then, in July 1915, as the organization's first vice-president.

Lovecraft saw amateurdom as a means to teach people to write properly and although he failed in this endeavor, he never stopped trying, championing the creation of the organization's Department of Instruction to teach aspiring writers the basics of grammar and versification and to direct people in their reading. He produced a prodigious quantity of work for amateur journalism between 1914 and 1921 and was still publishing articles and producing critical reviews in 1936. He edited around half a dozen magazines, as well as his own and became perhaps the best-known name in amateur journalism at the time.

Enlisting for the War

America entered the First World War on April 6, 1917. Lovecraft had longed for his country to take up arms alongside Britain for some time. Indeed, his love for England persuaded him to try to join the fray himself, a somewhat ludicrous notion, given his health and his life thus far. But, he wanted to support his beloved England and make something of himself:

'Some time ago, impressed by my entire uselessness in the world, I resolved to attempt enlistment despite my almost invalid condition. I argued that if I chose a regiment soon to depart for France, my sheer nervous force, which is not inconsiderable, might sustain me till a bullet or a piece of shrapnel could more conclusively & effectively dispose of me.'

A month after the declaration of war on Germany and her allies, therefore, he presented himself at the recruiting center for the Rhode Island National Guard. Amazingly, he was declared fit for service, no one having asked him about his previous mental health issues. He was enrolled in the 9th Coast Artillery, meaning that it was very unlikely that he would actually have been sent to Europe to fight.

Unfortunately, however, he had failed to inform his mother that he was enlisting and, as he put it, 'the sensation at home was far from slight'. In fact, when Susie found out she was hysterical and immediately set about getting him out.

Seeking the help of the family doctor and accompanied by him, she dragged Lovecraft back to the recruiting office where she informed the officers of their new recruit's breakdowns. Lovecraft's name was duly removed from the list. By this time, Lovecraft was 26 years of age, but, clearly, he was still firmly under his mother's thumb.

Susie's Health Deteriorates

Lovecraft had been living alone with his mother at 598 Angell Street since Whipple Phillips' death in 1904. His Aunt Annie was married and living in Cambridge, Massachusetts and his Aunt Lillian was also married and although still in Providence was living some distance away from Angell Street. Her husband, Franklin Chase Clark died in 1915.

In November 1918, Edwin, Susie's brother died and some suggest that her decline began then. To make matters worse, her and Howard's finances were seriously depleted by this time and the stress of constantly living on subsistence level must have also contributed to the decline in her mental wellbeing. Clara Hess revealed how bad things were:

'I remember that Mrs Lovecraft spoke to me about weird and fantastic creatures that rushed out from behind buildings and from corners at dark, and that she shivered and looked about apprehensively as she told her story. The last time I saw Mrs Lovecraft we were both going 'down street' on the Butler Avenue car. She was excited and apparently did not know where she was. She attracted the attention of everyone. I was greatly embarrassed, as I was the object of all her attention.'

Despair

It became obvious to everyone that Susie was very ill and on March 13, 1919, she was admitted to Butler Hospital, where her husband had died twenty-one years previously. She would remain there for two years until her death. His mother's absence impacted Lovecraft very badly, as he explained in a letter to his friend, Rheinhart Kleiner:

'... you above all others can imagine the effect of maternal illness & absence. I cannot eat, nor can I stay up long at a time. Pen-writing or typewriting nearly drives me insane. My nervous system seems to find its vent in feverish & incessant scribbling with a pencil ... She writes optimistic letters each day & I try to make my replies equally optimistic; though I do not find it possible to 'cheer up', eat, & go out, as she encourages me to do.'

A few weeks previously, as his mother's health rapidly worsened, Lovecraft had included a poem he had been writing in another letter to Kleiner. It was entitled *Despair* and is amongst the most affecting and powerful of all his poetic works:

THUS THE LIVING, LONE AND SOBBING,
IN THE THROES OF ANXIOUS THROBBING,
WITH THE LOATHSOME FURIES ROBBING
    NIGHT AND NOON OF PEACE AND REST
BUT BEYOND THE GROANS AND GRATING
OF ABHORRENT LIFE, IS WAITING
SWEET OBLIVION, CULMINATING
    ALL THE YEARS OF FRUITLESS QUEST.

Lovecraft with Rheinhart Kleiner, Providence, June 1919.

CHAPTER 3

BEYOND THE WALL OF SLEEP

Full of Nervous Fatigue

With his mother in hospital, Lovecraft was once again in the midst of a personal crisis that would forever change his life. When his grandmother died in 1896, the night-gaunts began to appear; when his father died in 1898, he experienced a 'near-breakdown'; when his grandfather died in 1904, he considered suicide. Other breakdowns or 'near-breakdowns' were the result of seemingly minor traumas such as attending school or learning to play the violin. He was now only spending three or four hours out of bed each day and was unable to deal with the large amount of amateur work that was falling through his letterbox.

His supposed ailments are mentioned continuously in his letters. He talks of turning down the editorship of the UAPA due to his 'ill health' and claims that his nervous system is 'a shattered wreck'. He had become fond of the notion that he was an invalid for whom the slightest act involved huge effort. But his ill health was undoubtedly psychosomatic, encouraged in his early life by his indulgent aunts and over-solicitous mother. Fellow UAPA member George Julian Houtain met Lovecraft in Boston in 1920 and reported:

'Lovecraft honestly believes he is not strong – that he has an inherited nervousness and fatigue wished upon him. One would never suspect in his massive form and well constructed body that there could be any ailment. To look at him one would think seriously before 'squaring off' ... It was never intended in the great scheme of things that such a magnificent physique should succumb to any mental dictation that commanded it to be subject to nervous ills and fatigue –

nor that that wonderful mentality should weakly and childishly listen to that – WHICH ISN'T.'

Venturing Out

Lovecraft visited his mother at the hospital but never went in because, needless to say, he had a phobia about hospitals. Even in the final stages of her illness when she was confined to her bed, he did not visit her which may not be as bad as it sounds because her illness was not believed to be life-threatening until just before she passed away. He soon accepted the fact that his mother was unlikely to return and eventually began to venture out.

He was now such a well-known figure in the world of amateur journalism that he was invited to conventions, both local and national. He may have appeared odd to the people he encountered at these affairs. One of them, Alfred Galpin described Lovecraft in those days, 'the strange half dead, half arrogant cock of his head weighed down by its enormous jaw, the rather fishy eyes ...'

Many noted the deathly pallor of his skin, the result of his years of only venturing out at night. They spoke of how stiffly he would sit at meetings, how he would stare straight ahead, his head turning only towards the person to whom he wished to speak. Nonetheless, his withdrawal from society was finally over.

In 1918, Lovecraft sold a story for the first time when the *National Magazine* purchased 'The Marshes of Ipswich'. Astonishingly, it was also the first money that he had earned in his entire life and he was by this time almost 30.

A Stupendous Monster of Nightmares

In November 1919, his first major story appeared in *The Vagrant*, published by W. Paul Cook, a man who would become important in Lovecraft's life. 'Dagon', written in 1917, around the same time as he wrote another story, 'The Tomb', elicited an enthusiastic response from readers despite protestations from Lovecraft that he was not 'a competent storyteller'.

'Dagon' was partly inspired from a dream Lovecraft had of which he said, 'I dreamed that whole hideous crawl, and can yet feel the ooze sucking me down!' It was also possibly influenced by the story 'Fishhead', written by Irvin S. Cobb, which was about a fish-shaped human.

'The Tomb', published in *The Vagrant* in March 1922, owes a great deal to Poe and to the Gothic tales that Lovecraft had devoured when younger. But 'Dagon', although also beholden to Poe with its first person narration and a gnawing fear that he wants to share, is different and begins to reach out for the style for which he would eventually become famous. It is leaner of language and leaves as a mystery the phenomena encountered by the narrator.

Under the Horned Waning Moon

Still uncertain whether fiction was the direction in which he wanted his writing to go, it took Lovecraft a year to turn out

DAGON

A seaman narrates how he is going to end his life once the morphine that has made life endurable runs out. He explains that during the First World War he was cast adrift in the Pacific after Germans captured his ship. His boat makes land on 'a slimy expanse of black mire' that he surmises was a piece of the ocean floor thrown to the surface. He walks for two days and comes upon an 'immeasurable pit or canyon' in the midst of which is a white monolith covered in images of 'fishes, eels, octopuses, crustaceans, mollusks, whales and the like.'

There are also images of human-like creatures but with webbed hands and feet, 'flabby lips, glassy, bulging eyes and other features less pleasant to recall'. Suddenly a huge creature emerges from the water, 'a stupendous monster of nightmares'. The narrator flees and the next thing he knows, he is in a San Francisco hospital, having been rescued in the middle of the Pacific by an American ship. He is haunted by visions of what he has seen but does not expect anyone to believe him. He fears for the future of mankind:

> *'I cannot think of the deep sea without shuddering at the nameless things that may at this very moment be crawling and floundering on its slimy bed, worshipping their ancient stone idols and carving their own detestable likenesses on submarine obelisks of water-soaked granite. I dream of a day when they may rise above the billows to drag down in their reeking talons the remnants of puny, war-exhausted mankind – of a day when the land shall sink, and the dark ocean floor shall ascend amidst universal pandemonium.'*

At the end of the story he hears 'a noise at the door, as of some immense slippery body lumbering against it,' and rushes to the window, presumably to throw himself out. His last terrified words are, 'It shall not find me. God, that hand! The window! The window!'

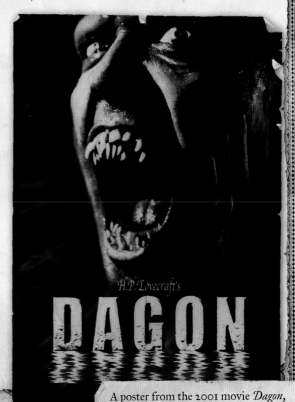

A poster from the 2001 movie *Dagon*, directed by Stuart Gordon.

Lovecraft, Charles W. Heins and W. Paul Cook, July 5, 1921.

another story. Like 'Dagon', 'Polaris' was inspired by a dream. 'Several nights ago,' he wrote to Maurice Winter Moe, 'I had a strange dream of a strange city – a city of many palaces and gilded domes, lying in a hollow betwixt ranges of grey, horrible hills ... I was, as I said, aware of this city visually. I was in it and around it. But certainly I had no corporeal existence.'

'Polaris' is a marvelous piece of prose-poetry. Very short, a mere 1,514 words long, its language echoes that of Lord Dunsany, even though he has not yet encountered the work of the Irish *fantaisiste*. It is the first of a series of stories that some have called the *Dreamlands* stories or the *Dream Cycle* that involve dreams. It is characterized by a great deal of carefully crafted descriptive detail, as in 'the red-leaved trees of the swamp mutter things to one another in the small hours of the morning under the horned waning moon' or 'the night of the great Aurora, when over the swamp played the shocking coruscations of the daemon-light' that hints at depths of mystery to which the reader is not party.

An Exceptionally Singular Dream

In 1918, Lovecraft collaborated with Winifred Virginia Jackson on a story entitled 'The Green Meadow' that would not, in fact, be published until 1927 in the final issue of W. Paul Cook's *The Vagrant*.

THE TOMB

A self-confessed dreamer named Jervas Dudley, discovers the entrance to a mausoleum as a child. It houses generations of the Hyde family whose nearby mansion burned down many years previously after being struck by lightning. Dudley is fascinated by the mausoleum but is unable to break the padlock on the door. He spends many nights sleeping outside the tomb and decides to wait until it is time to somehow force the lock.

Several years later, after awaking one afternoon with the feeling that a light has just been extinguished in the mausoleum, he goes to the attic of his house where he finds a key inside a rotting chest. He uses the key to open the padlock and enters the mausoleum.

He discovers an empty coffin with the name Jervas inscribed upon a plate on it and climbs into the coffin. He begins to sleep there every night and is changed by the experience:

> 'In the grey light of dawn I staggered from the vault and locked the chain of the door behind me. I was no longer a young man, though but twenty-one winters had chilled my bodily frame. Early-rising villagers who observed my homeward progress looked at me strangely, and marveled at the signs of ribald revelry which they saw in one whose life was known to be sober and solitary.'

One night he sees the Hyde mansion restored to its former glory with a party in progress. He joins in but lightning strikes the mansion, setting it on fire. Jervas loses consciousness, imagining himself being burned to death. He wakes up with two men restraining him, watched by his father. Meanwhile, a small box has been unearthed adorned with the initials 'J.H.' and a picture of someone that Jervas thinks is him.

His father tells him that they have known of his interest in the mausoleum, but explains that he has been watched and has never set foot inside, that the padlock is, in fact, rusty and has not been opened for decades. Jervas is then incarcerated in an asylum, presumed to have gone mad. He asks his servant to visit the mausoleum and he returns to tell him that inside there is indeed a coffin bearing the name 'Jervas'. In the final line he says he has been promised that he will be placed in that coffin on his death.

Cover of an *Adventure Comics* adaptation of 'The Tomb', 1991.

The story was based on a dream Jackson had, described by Lovecraft as 'exceptionally singular in that I had one exactly like it myself – save that mine did not extend so far. It was only when I had related my dream that Miss J. related the similar and more fully developed one. The opening paragraph of "The Green Meadow" was written for my own dream, but after hearing of the other, I incorporated it into the tale which I developed therefrom.'

Published under the pseudonyms Elizabeth Neville Berkeley and Lewis Theobald, Jun., it is not a story of any great quality.

An Increasing Sense of Dread

Another collaboration with Winifred Jackson, 'The Crawling Chaos', was completed in 1920. Lovecraft wrote all of the text from an idea that his writing partner came up with. It is a strange story. There is no

Winifred Virginia Jackson.

POLARIS

The story begins with the narrator describing the night sky and in particular Polaris the Pole Star 'winking hideously like an insane watching eye which strives to convey some strange message, yet recalls nothing save that it once had a message to convey'.

He goes on to tell of the night he first dreamt of a city of marble situated on a plateau between two 'strange peaks' while overhead 'glowed that watching Pole Star'. He sees men on the streets speaking in a language which, although he has never heard it before, he still seems to understand. He wakes up before he can find out any more, but dreams again and again of the strange marble city.

As time passes, he starts to wish he were part of the city and begins to question what constitutes reality and what constitutes dream. One night he finds himself in the city which he has now learned is 'Olathoë, lying on the plateau of Sarkis in the land of Lomar'. It is besieged by its enemy, the Inutos whom he describes as 'squat, hellish yellow fiends'.

The narrator describes himself as 'feeble and given to strange faintings when subjected to stress and hardships. But my eyes were the keenest in the city, despite the long hours I gave each day to the study of the Pnakotic manuscripts and the wisdom

of the Zobnarian Fathers' (here Lovecraft could be describing himself).

The narrator, like Lovecraft, is 'denied a warrior's part', being sent by his friend Alos, commander of the city's forces, to a watchtower to issue a signal if the Inutos gain entry to the city. Seeing Polaris in the night sky, he senses its malignant presence. He drifts off to sleep, thereby letting down his friend Alos by failing in his duty. He awakens back in his house but is now certain that his life is no more than a dream from which he cannot wake up. The Pole Star continues to twinkle malevolently:

'And as I writhe in my guilty agony, frantic to save the city whose peril every moment grows, and vainly striving to shake off this unnatural dream of a house of stone and brick south of a sinister swamp and a cemetery on a low hillock, the Pole Star, evil and monstrous, leers down from the black vault, winking hideously like an insane watching eye which strives to convey some message, yet recalls nothing save that it once had a message to convey.'

THE GREEN MEADOW

The introduction, written by Lovecraft, explains that the document that follows presents the contents of a notebook made of an unknown material embedded in a meteorite discovered in the sea off the Maine coast. The text is written in classical Greek by an ancient philosopher who had apparently escaped earth and journeyed to another planet.

The document itself tells of a person on a peninsula close to a rushing stream who has no idea who he or she is or how he got there. The peninsula breaks off and floats away on the river. In the distance is a green field that, the narrator claims, 'affected me badly'.

There is strange singing coming from it and as the narrator approaches he or she experiences an epiphany – 'therein was revealed all of which had puzzled me.' Then the text apparently becomes blurred and cannot be read any further. The prose is undoubtedly almost all Lovecraft's but the story is vague and dwindles away to nothing at the end.

plot, no drama, merely a series of images and descriptions and it feels more like a fragment of a story. The apocalyptic ending is well written, though, and almost worth waiting for. It was published in the April 1921 issue of *United Cooperative*.

Titanic Significance of Dreams

A slightly better effort also came in 1919. 'Beyond the Wall of Sleep' was the first in which Lovecraft introduced cosmic elements, his first science fiction tale, and, like 'The Tomb' and 'Polaris' it enters the world of dreams or visions.

The narrator says at the beginning of the story, 'I have frequently wondered if the majority of mankind ever pause to reflect upon the occasionally titanic significance of dreams, and of the obscure world to which they belong.' He suggests that when we are dreaming, we are actually 'sojourning in another and uncorporeal life of far different nature from the life we know.'

THE CRAWLING CHAOS

The narrator describes his sole experience with opium. He is administered an overdose by a doctor during the 'year of the plague'. He finds himself in a beautiful and exotic room but feels an increasing sense of dread, a fear of the unknown, compounded by the sound of loud pounding from outside. He flees, traveling inland and finding a valley in the center of which is a great palm tree. As he crawls towards it, an angelic-looking child tumbles out of its branches.

The child ominously says: 'It is the end. They have come down through the gloaming from the stars. Now all is over, and beyond the Arinurian streams we shall dwell blissfully in Teloe.'

Two youths appear, take the narrator by the hand and begin to describe the far-distant worlds of 'Teloe' and 'Cytharion of the Seven Suns' to him. By now, the narrator is floating high above the palm tree, accompanied by a number of singing youths who are wearing crowns of vines. They climb higher and the child tells the narrator that he should always look upward, never down at the earth far below. But, he

hears the sound of waves and does look back down at the earth where he witnesses destruction.

Cities are swept away by giant waves until there is nothing left. The waters drain into a hole on the earth's surface and then the entire world explodes:

'Then very suddenly it ended, and I knew no more till I awaked upon a bed of convalescence. As the cloud of steam from the Plutonic gulf finally concealed the entire surface from my sight, all the firmament shrieked at a sudden agony of mad reverberations which shook the trembling aether. In one delirious flash and burst it happened; one blinding, deafening holocaust of fire, smoke, and thunder that dissolved the wan moon as it sped outward to the void.

And when the smoke cleared away, and I sought to look upon the earth, I beheld against the background of cold, humorous stars only the dying sun and the pale mournful planets searching for their sister.'

'Beyond the Wall of Sleep' appeared in John Clinton Pryor's amateur magazine, *Pine Cones* in October 1919.

Exploring Future Themes

The stories Lovecraft wrote between 1917 and 1919 are extraordinarily diverse in theme. They also play with a variety of settings, tones and moods, as if Lovecraft was trying to discover the best direction in which to take his writing. In them he explores many of the themes that will be constant features in his work – the insignificance of mankind in the universe and its eventual extinction; dreams as a means of escaping to other realities; and the influence of the past on the present.

'Memory' is a prose poem in which a Daemon of the Valley converses with 'the Genie that haunts the moonbeams' and in which mankind has long been extinct – the first time Lovecraft deals with mankind's extinction.

'The Transition of Juan Romero', written in September 1916, tells the strange story of an incident at the Norton Mine when a vast cavern is opened up by blasting. During the night a loud throbbing emanates from the hole in the ground and Juan Romero who works at the mine disappears into it. An Englishman who is also working there looks over the edge and is horrified by what he sees. Unfortunately, however, Lovecraft does not share this vision with us – 'but God! I dare not tell you what I saw!' It is a confusing, vague and unsatisfying piece of work. Lovecraft did not particularly like it and withheld it from publication, even in amateur journals.

BEYOND THE WALL OF SLEEP

Joe Slater from the Catskill Mountains has been locked up in a mental hospital after committing a horrible murder. Slater is clearly insane, experiences weird cosmic visions and is unable to communicate properly. Fascinated by Slater's visions, the narrator, an intern at the hospital, creates a 'cosmic radio' that will enable him to share them.

In the night, the intern hears a voice. It transpires that throughout Slater's life, his body has been occupied by an extraterrestrial being of light that wants revenge on its nemesis – 'the oppressor' – near the star Algol. Slater is by this time dying and his demise will permit the being to extract its revenge. When he finally dies, there are reports of a new star close to Algol.

'On February 22, 1901, a marvelous new star was discovered by Dr. Anderson, of Edinburgh, not very far from Algol. No star had been visible at that point before. Within twenty-four hours the stranger had become so bright that it outshone Capella. In a week or two it had visibly faded, and in the course of a few months it was hardly discernible with the naked eye.'

Cover of an *Adventure Comics* adaptation of 'Beyond the Wall of Sleep', 1992.

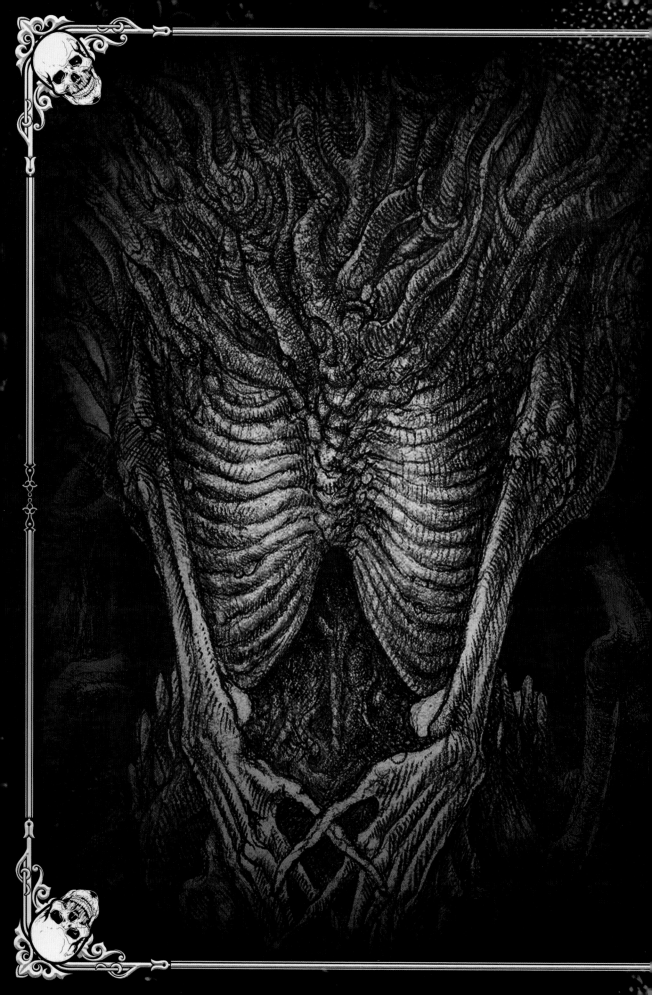

PART 2
THE DOOM THAT CAME TO SARNATH

CHAPTER 4

LORD DUNSANY & SONIA GREENE

The Irish Fantaisiste

In the autumn of 1919, Lovecraft discovered *A Dreamer's Tale*, a collection of stories by Lord Dunsany an Irish writer and dramatist noted for his short stories, mostly in the fantasy genre. His work would become Lovecraft's new obsession and a critical element in his development as a writer. He later wrote of his first encounter with Dunsany's work, 'The first paragraph arrested me as with an electrical shock.'

Lovecraft was smitten and for the next two years everything he wrote echoed the work of the Irish noble. This was not all bad, however,

as it gave him new ways to express himself and to convey his ideas. In fact, he must have found some familiarity in Dunsany's work as parts of it resembled the horrific dreams that he had experienced for years. He even went to Boston to hear the Irishman deliver a lecture on October 20, 1919. Under his influence, he went home and wrote the story 'The White Ship'. 'Celephaïs' followed the next year.

Dunsany was a remarkable character and it is easy to see how Lovecraft, with his love of the notion of the gentleman would become infatuated by him and his work. 'Dunsany is myself,' he would longingly say in a letter. He even wrote a fairly sycophantic and very

EDWARD PLUNKETT
18TH BARON OF DUNSANY

Born in London in 1878, Edward John Moreton Drax Plunkett, was educated at Eton and Sandhurst, became chess and pistol-shooting champion of Ireland, traveled widely and hunted. He fulfilled Lovecraft's idea of what a writer should be, writing not for money – he had plenty of that – but for pleasure. He served as a second lieutenant in the Coldstream Guards in the Second Boer War and while a captain in the Royal Inniskilling Fusiliers, he was wounded during the Easter Rising in 1916.

Written under the name Lord Dunsany, more than eighty books of his work were published, and his oeuvre includes many hundreds of short stories, as well as successful plays, novels and essays.

Dunsany lived much of his life at what may be Ireland's longest-inhabited house, Dunsany Castle near Tara. He worked with W.B. Yeats and Lady Gregory and received an honorary doctorate from Trinity College, Dublin. He died in Dublin in 1957, aged 79, after an attack of appendicitis.

Edward Plunkett, 18th Baron of Dunsany.

bad poem to him that was published in the amateur magazine, the *Tryout*, and was sent to the writer by a friend of Lovecraft. Dunsany replied graciously, thanking Lovecraft for his 'warm and generous enthusiasm, crystallized in verse'.

Dunsany's influence on Lovecraft is evident in a series of stories that Lovecraft wrote around this time – 'The White Ship', 'The Doom that Came to Sarnath', 'The Statement of Randolph Carter', written in 1919; 'The Cats of Ulthar' and 'Celephaïs', written in 1920; and 'The Quest of Iranon', written in 1921. There are many Dunsanian elements – long convoluted sentences, the unbridled use of semi-colons and descriptions of mythical cities filled with fabulous wonders that are viewed from afar by protagonists who rarely enter them. There are suggestions of knowledge and science that is beyond the understanding of mere mortals. One difference, however, is that Lovecraft's visions were often taken directly from the terrifying dreams he had.

Dunsany is Myself

'The White Ship' is a distinctly Dunsanian piece of writing, as he candidly admitted in a letter to his friend Kleiner. If there is a moral to the story, it is that you should not abandon tranquility, as embodied by Sona-Nyl, because a terrible fate awaits, bringing sadness and misery.

'The White Ship' had first appeared in the *United Amateur* in November 1919 and was warmly received by Alfred Galpin, the head of the organization's Department of Public Criticism. He praised Lovecraft's decision to write fiction and the story itself: 'The lover of dream literature will find all he might long for in the carefully sustained poetry of language, the simple narration, and the profound inner harmonies of "The White Ship".'

Descended from the Moon

The next tale in a Dunsanian mold by Lovecraft, 'The Doom that Came to Sarnath' was written on December 3, 1919. It is less complex and philosophical than 'The White Ship' and, in fact, is just a good tale well written. It is not the last we hear of Sarnath from Lovecraft. It is mentioned in 'The Quest of Iranon' and in 'The Nameless City' and the city of Ib also reappears in Lovecraft's novella, *At the Mountains of Madness*.

'The Doom that Came to Sarnath' first saw the light of day in a Scottish amateur journal, *The Scot* in June 1920.

THE WHITE SHIP

This philosophical allegory tells the story of Basil Elton, a lighthouse keeper. A bearded man in robes navigates a mysterious white ship when the moon is full. Elton boards the ship after walking out across the water on a bridge of moonbeams. The ship sails off, led by an azure celestial bird, to a mystical chain of islands that are different to any place on earth – Zar 'where dwell all the dreams and thoughts of beauty that come to men once and then are forgotten'; Thalarion, 'the City of a Thousand Wonders, wherein reside all those mysteries that man has striven in vain to fathom'; Xura, 'the Land of Pleasures Unattained'; and Sona-Nyl, where 'there is neither time nor space, neither suffering or death.'

Elton spends what he claims are 'many aeons' in Sona-Nyl but eventually longs to return to Cathuria, the Land of Hope, a place that he believes to be even more wonderful. The bearded captain of the ship reluctantly agrees to take him there. They discover, however, that out beyond the basalt pillars of the West where Cathuria should lie is a 'monstrous cataract' into the 'abysmal nothingness' of which the oceans of the world fall. The White Ship plummets to its doom and is destroyed.

Elton wakes up on the rocks beside his lighthouse and only a few moments have passed, it seems, since he departed on the ship. As he opens his eyes he sees a ship being wrecked on the rocks as a result of his having neglected to switch on the light. Next morning, nothing remains of the shipwreck apart from the corpse of a bird that looks like the one the White Ship had followed on its journey, and a single, brilliant white wooden spar. The White Ship never appears to him again.

THE DOOM THAT CAME TO SARNATH

This is the story of the land of Mnar. Ten thousand years ago, the banks of the River Ai were colonized by a race of shepherd people who built the cities of Thraa, Ilarnek and Kadatheron which became powerful both in terms of trade and intellectual achievement. A group of inhabitants went off in search of more land, settling on the shores of a huge lake, in a place that they called Sarnath.

Across the lake from them was a settlement, 'the grey stone city of Ib, peopled by a race that had descended from the moon, in hue as green as the lake and the mists that rise above it … They had bulging eyes, pouting, flabby lips, and curious ears, and were without voice.' They worship the god Bokrug, the Great Water Lizard. The people of Sarnath slaughter the other race, capturing the idol of their god as a trophy but the following night the idol vanishes amidst strange occurrences – 'weird lights were seen over the lake.' Taran-Ish, their high priest is found dead but before he died, he had scrawled 'DOOM' on the altar. A thousand years later, while Sarnath was at the height of its power, a celebration was held to commemorate the destruction of Ib and nobles from distant cities were invited to a great feast.

That night, however, strange lights were once again seen over the lake and dense fog blanketed the area. The water of the lake rises almost submerging the granite tidal marker. Terrified, the inhabitants of the city flee, some reporting that they had seen the long-dead inhabitants of Ib peering from the windows of the city's towers while others were too dumbstruck to recount what they have seen.

When they return they find the city in ruins and inhabited by countless water lizards. Strangest of all, the idol that had disappeared all those centuries ago was back:

> 'Where once had risen walls of three hundred cubits and towers yet higher, now stretched only the marshy shore, and where once had dwelt fifty million of men now crawled the detestable water-lizard. Not even the mines of precious metal remained. DOOM had come to Sarnath.'

Blighted by Terrible Dreams

Meanwhile, Lovecraft's nights were still blighted by terrible dreams, one of which provided him with the elements of his next story, 'The Statement of Randolph Carter', written in December 1919 and first published in *The Vagrant* in May 1920. In a letter to August Derleth of December 11, 1919, Lovecraft admitted that the story was basically a transcription of the dream in which he and his close friend Samuel Loveman visit an ancient cemetery where Loveman suffers a hideous but unknown fate after climbing down into a crypt.

Carter would become a recurring Lovecraft character, appearing in a further four stories – 'The Unnamable', *The Dream-Quest of Unknown Kadath*, 'The Silver Key' and 'Through the Gates of the Silver Key', written in collaboration with E. Hoffman Price.

Lovecraft outside 598 Angell Street, Providence, June 1919.

THE STATEMENT OF RANDOLPH CARTER

The story is narrated in the first person in the form of a witness statement to the police and is told by Randolph Carter who has been found wandering through swampland in shock and having lost his memory. His statement is an explanation of what has happened to his friend, the occultist, Harley Warren, who has suffered the same fate as Loveman in Lovecraft's dream.

Warren, it transpires, possesses a number of 'strange, rare books on forbidden subjects' some of which are written in Arabic. One book in particular he forbids Carter from reading but tells him that he has worked out from it that there exist doors and stairways between the surface of the earth and the underworld through which demons can pass. He persuades Carter to visit an ancient graveyard near Big Cypress Swamp that marks the site of one such portal.

On arriving, Warren pinpoints one particular tomb and on opening it, finds a staircase that descends into the depths. He picks up a lantern and starts down the stairs, leaving Carter on the surface but communicating with him by means of a telephone wire. Suddenly, after a period of silence, Carter hears panicked sounds on the telephone. Carter explains what happened next:

Over and over again through those eons I whispered and muttered, called, shouted, and screamed, 'Warren! Warren! Answer me are you there?' ... I do not try, gentlemen, to account for that thing – that voice – nor can I venture to describe it in detail, since the first words took away my consciousness and created a mental blank which reaches to the time of my awakening in the hospital. Shall I say that the voice was deep; hollow; gelatinous; remote; unearthly; inhuman; disembodied? What shall I say? It was the end of my experience, and is the end of my story. I heard it, and knew no more – heard it as I sat petrified in that unknown cemetery in the hollow, amidst the crumbling stones and the falling tombs, the rank vegetation and the miasmal vapors – heard it well up from the innermost depths of that damnable open sepulchre as I watched amorphous, necrophagous shadows dance beneath an accursed waning moon.

And this is what it said: 'You fool, Warren is DEAD!'

Throwing Off the Dunsanian Shackles

Around the start of 1920, Lovecraft very much signaled his intention to concentrate on fiction rather than poetry by beginning a commonplace book, its purpose described by him as follows: 'This book consists of ideas, images & quotations hastily jotted down for possible future use in weird fiction. Very few are actually developed plots – for the most part they are merely suggestions or random impressions designed to set the memory or imagination working. Their sources are various – dreams, things read, casual incidents, idle conceptions, & so on.' As has been shown by assiduous scholarship on the part of David E. Schultz in his now unavailable annotated version of the commonplace book, the 222 entries in this book all contributed to Lovecraft's future output of fiction and also informed some of his weird poetry.

Dunsany still featured large in Lovecraft's writing at the start of 1920 and it would not be until the middle of the year that he would shrug off his Dunsanian shackles, in a story entitled 'The Temple'. His stories until this time had been relatively short, weighing in, on average, at around 2,500 words, but 'The Temple', at 6,000 words was his longest tale to date.

Into the Great Unknown

In 'The Temple', Lovecraft finds a motif that will be ever-present in his later work – the existence of a great and unknown human civilization. In fact, both human and extraterrestrial civilizations feature in many of his stories, cultures that were growing long before our own. The fact that such wondrous and sophisticated civilizations could emerge and then disappear from history proves the transitory nature of our own world. Of course, in 'The Temple' the fact that there appears to be light emanating from the object of Altberg's fascination would suggest that perhaps the ancient civilization that created 'Atlantis' has not entirely died out and is awaiting an opportunity to rise up and seize the earth for itself once again.

Contemporary in nature with its First World War setting, some elements of 'The Temple' jar with the reader, in particular some of the words that Lovecraft puts into the mouth of the German U-Boat commander. Statements such as 'our victorious German exploits', 'our great German nation, my iron German will' render Altberg fairly ridiculous and make him appear like a caricature of a German naval man.

The story itself is flawed. There are a number of incidents that are unexplained and do not seem to have any connection to the temple. The British sailor who clung to the rails, for instance, is seen swimming away from the submarine once his hands have been freed. What is the relevance of the dolphins that swim at unaccustomed depths and for unusually lengthy periods? Of course, these elements add to the overall atmosphere of weirdness and unease and this may simply have been what Lovecraft was aiming for. Nonetheless, they leave unanswered questions in the reader's mind.

'The Temple' was a story that Lovecraft liked but it did not appear in any amateur journals, probably because of its length. It was first published in *Weird Tales* in September 1925.

If Separate Species We Be

In the autumn of 1920, Lovecraft wrote 'Facts Concerning the Late Arthur Jermyn and His Family', a story with more restrained language than hitherto. It tells of the reason for Arthur Jermyn's self-immolation.

The story begins with one of the most famous passages in Lovecraft's writings:

> *'Life is a hideous thing, and from the background behind what we know of it peer daemoniacal hints of truth which make it sometimes a thousandfold more hideous.*

> *Science, already oppressive with its shocking revelations, will perhaps be the ultimate exterminator of our human species – if separate species we be – for its reserve of unguessed horrors could never be borne by mortal brains if loosed upon the world.'*

In saying 'if separate species we be', Lovecraft is suggesting that human beings may not be entirely 'human'. Later in the story, he describes the 'prehistoric *white* Congolese civilization':

> *'Especially was it unwise to rave of the living things that might haunt such a place; of creatures half of the jungle and half of the impiously aged city – fabulous creatures which even a Pliny might describe with skepticism; things that might have sprung up after the great apes had overrun the dying city with the walls and the pillars, the vaults and the weird carvings.'*

These creatures, Lovecraft is suggesting, are the missing link between the apes and humans and are where the human race came from, a notion to which Lovecraft's racist attitude would certainly take exception, were it suggested to him in real life. Thus, the story is suggesting that humanity emerged from this primitive race in Africa, but it was a race corrupted by breeding with apes.

Of course, this story is about more than an unholy marriage. It betrays Lovecraft's racism. The ape is a thinly veiled reference to black people and, as we know, Lovecraft believed black people to be racially inferior to whites and especially the Anglo-Saxon settlers who had come to New England.

'Facts Concerning the Late Arthur Jermyn and His Family' was written for serialization in Horace L. Wilson's *Wolverine*, appearing in the March and June issues in 1921. In *The Vivisector* of November 1921, it received praise from Lovecraft's young friend, Alfred Galpin who claimed that the story showed 'another phase of [Lovecraft's] gloomy but powerful genius. It is perfect in execution, restrained in manner, complete and marked by Mr Lovecraft's uniquely effective handling

THE TEMPLE

The story is in the guise of a 'found manuscript' written by Karl Heinrich Graf von Altberg-Ehrenstein, a lieutenant-commander in the German Navy during the First World War. He declares that he wants to reveal the events leading to his final hour in a submarine at the bottom of the sea. He describes events between June and August 1917 when his U-Boat, U-29, sank SS *Victory*, a British freighter and then sank the lifeboats in which its crew had fled the sinking ship. Altberg, a cruel and arrogant man, orders his vessel to submerge and when it finally surfaces again, they find the body of a British seaman who had drowned clinging to the submarine's railings.

On the body the crew discovers a strange piece of carved ivory. Thinking it might be valuable, one of them keeps it but soon strange things begin to happen. The submarine is dragged southward by a previously unknown current while several members of the crew begin to suffer from exhaustion and have dreadful nightmares. When one crew member describes seeing the corpses of the drowned British sailors staring in through the portholes of the submarine, Altberg has him chained up and whipped.

Meanwhile, the other members of the crew plead with Altberg to throw the ivory charm overboard, becoming irrational due to sheer terror and Altberg orders a couple of them to be executed to help maintain discipline. Suddenly, there is an explosion that damages the vessel's engines. They have lost the ability to navigate and can only surface and dive. When a United States warship appears, several crew members plead with Altberg to surrender but he has them killed.

Later, in the grip of a violent storm, he orders the submarine to submerge but finds that it is now unable to surface. The six crewmen who remain attempt a mutiny, screaming about the ivory talisman and destroying the submarine's instruments, but Altberg kills them all, leaving alive on board only him and his fellow officer, Lieutenant Klenze. The submarine drifts aimlessly with Altberg and Klenze sweeping the vessel's powerful searchlight across the murky depths, watching dolphins following them. Klenze eventually loses his mind:

It was at 3:15 p.m., August 12, that poor Klenze went wholly mad. He had been in the conning tower using the searchlight when I saw him bound into the library compartment where I sat reading,

and his face at once betrayed him. I will repeat here what he said, underlining the words he emphasized: 'He is calling! He is calling! I hear him! We must go!' As he spoke he took his ivory image from the table, pocketed it, and seized my arm in an effort to drag me up the companionway to the deck. In a moment I understood that he meant to open the hatch and plunge with me into the water outside, a vagary of suicidal and homicidal mania for which I was scarcely prepared. As I hung back and attempted to soothe him he grew more violent, saying: 'Come now – do not wait until later; it is better to repent and be forgiven than to defy and be condemned.' Then I tried the opposite of the soothing plan, and told him he was mad – pitifully demented. But he was unmoved, and cried: 'If I am mad, it is mercy! May the gods pity the man who in his callousness can remain sane to the hideous end! Come and be mad whilst he still calls with mercy!'

Altberg opens the airlock and Klenze drifts through it to his death, bearing the ivory charm. A couple of days later, the U-Boat finally settles on the ocean floor. In front of him Altberg is astonished to see the ruins of an ancient city. He decides that it must be the mythical city of Atlantis and climbs into a diving suit to explore its buildings. One building, a temple, holds a strange fascination for him, and he longs to explore its interior, although fears what he might find. The next day he comes to a terrifying realization:

The head of the radiant god in the sculptures on the rock temple is the same as that carven bit of ivory which the dead sailor brought from the sea and which poor Klenze carried back into the sea.

He sees a glow in the water and has an 'aural delusion', hearing the sound of 'some wild yet beautiful chant or choral hymn' coming from outside the submarine. Climbing up to the conning tower, he sees the doors and windows of the temple 'aglow with a flickering radiance, as from a mighty altar-flame far within'. Even with his 'German will', he can no longer resist the visions and hallucinations and is drawn to go inside the temple. Before he willingly goes to his death, he places the manuscript in a bottle and sends it to the surface. It will later be found on a beach in Yucatan.

of introductory and concluding portions ... [it] does not derive from Poe, Dunsany, or any other of Mr Lovecraft's favorites and predecessors.'

Galpin was a young prodigy that Lovecraft had taken under his wing, considering him an 'honorary grandson'. It was Galpin who introduced Lovecraft to the thinking of the German philosopher, Friedrich Nietzsche and the work of American fantasy author, sculptor and painter, Clark Ashton Smith.

The Death of Susie Lovecraft

Susie Lovecraft died in Butler Hospital on May 24, 1921 of complications arising from gall-bladder surgery. Naturally, Lovecraft was devastated but even in death she cast a huge shadow over his life. He wrote not long after her passing: 'My mother was, in all probability, the only person who thoroughly understood me ... I shall not again be likely to meet with a mind so thoroughly admirable.' With her gone, suicide seemed to be a viable option for him. 'During my mother's lifetime I was aware that voluntary euthanasia on my part would cause her distress, but it is now possible for me to regulate the term of my existence with the assurance that my end would cause no one more than a passing annoyance.' He did little in the weeks following, becoming listless and merely drifting through life.

LEFT: Alfred Galpin.
RIGHT: Friedrich Nietzsche in 1869.

But, much as he thought about it and even discussed methods with friends, he never attempted to kill himself.

In fact, he soon began to lift himself out of his despair, realizing that for the first time in his life he was free to do as he pleased, that he did not have to take into account anyone else's feelings. He began to take trips around New England, dropping in on amateurs with whom he had been corresponding and searching out historic sights. He even attended some amateur writing conventions. Interestingly, several of the amateurs he visited were single women.

One of these women was Myrta Little, a former college professor, just two years older than Lovecraft, who was launching a career as an amateur writer and lived in Hampstead, New Hampshire. He met her on June 8, 1921, his aunts, hoping for an end to Lovecraft's bachelordom, had encouraged him to arrange it. They met again in New Hampshire in August. Nothing ever came of their acquaintance but Lovecraft, it seemed, may have been searching for a woman to replace his mother.

FACTS CONCERNING THE LATE ARTHUR JERMYN AND HIS FAMILY

An eighteenth century ancestor of Arthur Jermyn, Sir Wade Jermyn, had been 'one of the earliest explorers of the Congo region' but had been sent to an asylum after speaking about a prehistoric Congolese civilization.

Sir Wade had brought back a wife from the Congo. It was said that she was the daughter of a Portuguese trader but no one ever saw her and the children the couple had were odd in both looks and mentality. In the middle of the following century, another ancestor, Sir Robert Jermyn, had murdered his entire family as well as a fellow African explorer that had brought back from Africa strange stories from the area where Sir Wade Jermyn had carried out his work.

In order to clear the family name, Arthur Jermyn, who is himself strange in appearance, tries to continue Sir Wade's research. In 1912, while investigating a story of a white ape that became a goddess in the prehistoric Congolese civilization, he finds the remains of the site of the civilization, but there is nothing to prove the existence of the white ape. He hears that the body of the white ape has been stuffed but has disappeared. A Belgian agent he meets offers to find the stuffed goddess and ship it to him. Jermyn returns to England and after some months the body of the white ape is delivered to his house. Opening the crate, he makes a dreadful discovery:

'Arthur Jermyn dismissed everyone from the room before opening the box, though the instant sound of hammer and chisel showed that he did not delay the operation. Nothing was heard for some time; just how long Soames cannot exactly estimate, but it was certainly less than a quarter of an hour later that the horrible scream, undoubtedly in Jermyn's voice, was heard. Immediately afterward Jermyn emerged from the room, rushing frantically toward the front of the house as if pursued by some hideous enemy. The expression on his face, a face ghastly enough in repose, was beyond description. When near the front door he seemed to think of something, and turned back in his flight, finally disappearing down the stairs to the cellar. The servants were utterly dumbfounded, and watched at the head of the stairs, but their master did not return.'

In the cellar, Jermyn covers himself in oil and sets himself alight. 'A spark appeared on the moor, a flame arose, and a pillar of human fire reached to the heavens.'

It transpires that the ape had been wearing a locket around her neck with the Jermyn coat of arms engraved on it. Moreover, she bears a striking resemblance to Arthur Jermyn. Sir Wade Jermyn's wife was not the daughter of a Portuguese trader but was instead an ape goddess. Arthur Jermyn and all the other descendants of Sir Wade were the result of that union.

SONIA GREENE

Sonia Haft Greene was born Sonia Haft Shafirkin in 1883 in Ichnya near Kiev in the Ukraine. Her father died when she was a child and her mother emigrated with Sonia and her brother. Leaving the children in Liverpool, she went on to America where she re-married. Sonia joined her a year later and in 1899, aged 16, married a 26-year-old man named Samuel Seckendorff. The couple's son, born in 1900, died at 3 months old but in 1902 they had a daughter named Florence. Sonia's husband died in 1916 perhaps having committed suicide but before that, he had changed his family's name to Greene.

She worked in an executive position, specializing in hats, with Ferle Heller's, a women's clothing outlet on Fifth Avenue and is reputed to have earned the respectable wage of $10,000 a year. She lived in the fashionable area of Flatbush in Brooklyn, New York and was described by Lovecraft's friend Rheinhart Kleiner as physically very attractive. Lovecraft's friend, Alfred Galpin gives a more fulsome description:

'When she dropped in on my reserved and bookish life at Madison, I felt like an English sparrow transfixed by a cobra. Junoesque and commanding, with superb dark eyes and hair, she was too regal to be a Dostoievski character and seemed rather a heroine from some of the most martial pages of War and Peace. Proclaiming the glory of the free and enlightened human personality, she declared herself a person unique in depth and intensity of passion and urged me to "Write, to Do, to Create".'

She had been brought into the amateur fold by James F. Morton and was very taken by the amateur cause, contributing the princely sum of 50 dollars to the Official Organ Fund. Lovecraft acknowledged this donation in the September 1921 United Amateur, describing her act as an 'example of amateur devotion and enthusiasm which should be heeded by all members as an inspiration to renewed activity'.

He was slightly less restrained in a letter he wrote around this time:

'Some liberality! Upon sending in her United application, and merely after having read a few stray papers and old official organs, Mme Greene unsolicitedly and unexpectedly came across with a pledge of FIFTY (count 'em – 50!) refulgent rubles – HALF A HUNDRED scintillant simoleons – for the Official Organ Fund. Ten of 'em cash down. Oh boy! Is that the ideal amateur spirit? We'll notify the cosmos!'

Lovecraft and Sonia Greene, Boston, July 5, 1921.

Encountering Sonia Greene

On July 4, 1921, he met another woman. He was introduced to her by his friend Rheinhart Kleiner at the National Press Association's annual convention in Boston. It was Sonia Greene.

Sonia immediately showed a great deal of interest in Lovecraft, seeking out anyone who knew him. She admits that on her first meeting she 'admired his personality but frankly, at first, not his person.' Admittedly, he was no oil painting, in his out-of-date clothing, with his lantern jaw, plain looks and persistent skin problems. Nonetheless, the two began to write to each other. As for Lovecraft, he seems to have been impressed by her 'acute, receptive and well-stored mind'.

It would probably have remained nothing more than a correspondence between two amateur writers if Sonia had not decided to seize the initiative by paying a visit to Lovecraft in Providence on September 4 – 5, taking a room at the Crown Hotel. He showed her the sights of Providence and back at 598 Angell Street, introduced her to his Aunt Lillian. Sonia invited Lovecraft and his aunt to dinner at her hotel but Lillian had eaten lunch that day and declined the invitation. Lovecraft accepted but ate only ice cream and drank a coffee.

The following day, the tour of Providence's treasures continued and then he and Lillian had lunch with Sonia at the Crown. By this time, Lovecraft was quite smitten. 'Mme. G. is certainly a person of admirable qualities, whose generous and kindly cast of mind is by no means feigned, and whose intelligence and devotion to art merit the sincerest appreciation. The volatility incidental to a Continental and non-Aryan heritage should not blind the analytical observer to the solid work and genuine cultivation which underlie it.' Praise indeed!

Sonia launched her own amateur magazine, *Rainbow*, in October 1921 to which Lovecraft and his circle contributed.

Earning a Living

With his small inheritance dwindling, Lovecraft began to look around for some means of earning an income. A man named David van Bush appeared on the scene and provided him with a temporary solution. Bush self-published a variety of books – poetry, psychology, mind, body, spirit and aspirational. He engaged Lovecraft, along with others, to edit his work. Bush was popular and, as well as writing, gave public lectures. But the editing was tough and gave Lovecraft terrible headaches. 'I have just emerged from a veritable "killer", contracted by working half the forenoon and all the afternoon on Bush junk,' he wrote. Nonetheless, Bush was a regular client and he paid well, a dollar for 48 lines of verse in 1920 and by 1922 a dollar for every 8 lines. This when *Weird Tales* was only paying Lovecraft 25 cents a line. It was around this time, however, that Lovecraft's career as a professional writer of fiction began.

Lovecraft on the shore in Magnolia, Massachusetts, August 1922.

Herbert West – Reanimator

Home Brew was a magazine started by NAPA's former president, George Julian Houtain, in 1921. He commissioned Lovecraft to write a series of horror stories for payment of 5 dollars a story, the first time Lovecraft received payment for prose fiction work. Although each story could be read on its own, they were, effectively, six chapters of one story that Lovecraft named 'Herbert West – Reanimator'.

Begun in September 1921, he completed the last chapter in April or May of 1922. It is notable as the first piece of his fiction in which he mentions his fictional Miskatonic University but Lovecraft also presents one of the first depictions of zombie-like creatures as corpses that have been reanimated scientifically. Each chapter ended with a cliffhanger – an unfamiliar narrative technique for Lovecraft – and each new chapter had to begin with a recap of what has occurred in previous chapters.

'Herbert West – Reanimator' was described as 'wretched work' by the book *Science Fiction – The Early Years* and the great Lovecraft scholar, S.T. Joshi, has said that the story is 'universally acknowledged as Lovecraft's poorest work'. It may be that Lovecraft did not enjoy writing the chapters, especially as he was being paid to do so, running contrary to his belief that writing should be a gentlemanly profession and that no money should change hands in order to bring a literary work into being:

'My sole inducement is the monetary reward, which is a guinea per tale,' he wrote, 'Now this is manifestly inartistic. To write to order, to drag one figure through a series of artificial episodes, involves the violation of all that spontaneity and singleness of impression that should characterize short story work. It reduces the unhappy author from art to the commonplace level of mechanical and unimaginative hack-work. Nevertheless, when one needs the money one is not scrupulous – so I have accepted the job!'

Haunted and Driven Mad

Inspiration for the story came from Mary Shelley's great Gothic novel *Frankenstein, or the Modern Prometheus*. The narrator is a doctor who had attended medical school with the Herbert West of the title at Miskatonic University in the fictional town of Arkham where many of Lovecraft's stories would be set. West has disappeared after developing a serum that when injected into a corpse, brings it back to life, or at least a horrific semblance of life. By the end of the tale, the narrator is haunted, believed to have been driven mad by his knowledge of the reanimated corpses.

Lovecraft hated Houtain's magazine, especially as his story had been re-named by the editor as 'Grewsome Tales' which was not at all to Lovecraft's liking. Houtain was very enthusiastic, however, stating on the magazine's cover that "Grewsome Tales' is better than Edgar Allen [*sic*] Poe'.

Lovecraft was at the same time collaborating with other writers. He worked with some young authors, editing and revising their work, because he saw promise in them, but he also worked with others purely for money. Some of this work was well below the standard that was acceptable to Lovecraft but he dealt with them politely. In private, however, he was less than polite:

'When I revised the kindergarten pap and idiot-asylum slop of other fishes, I was, in a microscopic way, putting just the faintest bit of order, coherence, direction and comprehensible language into something whose Neanderthaloid ineptitude was already mapped out. My work, ignominious as it was, was at least in the right direction – making that which was utterly amorphous and drooling just the minutest trifle less close to the protozoan stage.'

(Right) The cover of *Weird Tales*, March 1942, featuring 'Herbert West: Reanimator' was by Hannes Bok, the pseudonym of American artist and illustrator Wayne Woodard (1914 – 1964). During his career, Bok produced nearly 150 covers for various science fiction, fantasy, and detective fiction magazines, as well as contributing hundreds of black and white interior illustrations.

HELL ON EARTH — A Novelette of Satan in a Tuxedo — By ROBERT BLOCH

MARCH

Weird Tales

15¢

A NEW
LOVECRAFT
SERIES . . .
Herbert West: Reanimator

THE RAT MASTER
Greye La Spina

FRANK OWEN   MALCOLM JAMESON

The original story of 'Herbert West – Reanimator', may not have been one of Lovecraft's greatest, but when Stuart Gordon made it into a science fiction movie in 1985, *Re-animator* became something of a cult classic. (Above) Bruce Abbott has lost his head in a scene from the movie, which mixes extreme gore, horror and comedy. (Right) Lobby card/poster.

CHAPTER 5

NEW YORK SOJOURN

Branching Out with Sonia

In 1922, H.P. Lovecraft left New England for the first time, spending from April 6 to 12 in New York, at the behest of Sonia Greene who had met fellow amateurs and Lovecraft associates, Samuel Loveman and Alfred Galpin, while on a business trip to Chicago. She had long wanted to get together all of Lovecraft's friends in New York and get the great man to come and spend time with them. She persuaded Loveman to move to New York and he had arrived on April 1, 1922. Lovecraft had been corresponding with Loveman for some time but had never met him. Therefore, Sonia suggested he come to the city to meet him.

His other friends, Morton and Kleiner also urged Lovecraft to make the five-hour train journey to the city. Another Lovecraft associate that he had never met, Frank Belknap Long (1901 – 94) was also going to be there.

On April 6, Lovecraft boarded the 10.06 train from Providence to Penn station. The visit was filled with discussion, visits to museums, galleries and bookshops and sightseeing. He and Loveman slept in Sonia's apartment while she slept in a neighbour's apartment.

He was particularly pleased to meet Loveman and Long at last and spent a good deal of time with Sonia. She took him to his first Italian restaurant and introduced him to her daughter Florence but Lovecraft was not taken with her – a 'pert, spoiled and ultra-independent infant rather more hard-boiled of visage than her benignant mater' was how he described her.

In New York, unfortunately, his rampant racism came to the surface:

'We walked – at my suggestion – in the middle of the street, for contact with the heterogeneous sidewalk denizens, spilled out of their bulging brick kennels as if by a

SAMUEL LOVEMAN

For the first 37 years of his life, poet, critic and dramatist, Samuel Loveman, lived and worked in Cleveland. He published many poems between 1905 and 1908 and then between 1919 and 1926 in amateur publications. He moved to New York around the same time as his friend, the poet Hart Crane, and worked as a bookseller. He began corresponding with Lovecraft in 1917 and was close to him during the short period when Lovecraft lived in New York. Lovecraft wrote the poem 'To Samuel Loveman, Esquire, on His Poetry and Drama, Writ in the Elizabethan style' and 'The Statement of Randolph Carter' and the prose poem 'Nyarlathotep' were based on dreams of Lovecraft's in which Loveman featured. Loveman worked in the book trade until relatively old and died in obscurity in an old people's home in 1976, aged 89.

Samuel Loveman

FRANK BELKNAP LONG

Frank Belknap Long was a prolific writer in a number of genres – horror, fantasy, science fiction, poetry, gothic romance, comic books and non-fiction. Born in Manhattan in 1901, he developed an interest in the weird by reading Frank Baum's *Oz* books, Jules Verne, H.G. Wells, Ambrose Bierce and Edgar Allan Poe. He was first published in *United Amateur* in 1920. Lovecraft enjoyed his work and began a correspondence with Long that endured until Lovecraft's death in 1937.

He studied journalism and resolved to become a freelance writer, selling his first story to *Weird Tales* in 1922. For the ensuing four decades, he was a frequent contributor to pulp magazines, including *Weird Tales* and *Astounding Science Fiction*. In the 1940s, Long wrote comic books and scripts for *Planet Comics*, *Superman*, *Congo Bill*, DC's *Green Lantern* and Fawcett Comics' *Captain Marvel*. In the 1950s, he edited a number of magazines. When the pulps began to disappear, the ever-versatile Long began to write science fiction and gothic romance novels.

He died in 1994 at the age of 92, and was so poor that his remains were interred in a pauper's grave. When his friends and associates learned of this, they had him exhumed and re-buried at New York's Woodlawn Cemetery in a family plot not far from the graves of Lovecraft's grandparents. He had written 29 novels, 150 stories, eight collections of short stories, three volumes of poetry and countless magazine articles and comic strips.

Lovecraft and Frank Belknap Long in Brooklyn, July 11, 1931.

spawning beyond the capacity of the places, was by no means to be sought. At times, though, we struck particularly deserted areas – these swine have instinctive swarming movements, no doubt which no ordinary biologist can fathom. Gawd knows what they are ... a bastard mess of stewing mongrel flesh without intellect, repellent to eye, nose, and imagination – would to heaven a kindly gust of cyanide would asphyxiate the whole gigantic abortion, end the misery, and clean out the place.'

Going Back in Time

In May 1922, Lovecraft visited Myrta Little again and was driven by Sonia to Dover which was the furthest north he had ever been. He was deeply impressed by this car journey:

'... a trip back through Time, extending 75 to 200 years, and plunging me into the heart of an ancient New-England which I had mourned as dead and buried. Words cannot convey the charms of the winding, hilly road; the placid pastoral panoramas at every turn; the magic glimpses of cool centuried farmhouses amidst old gardens and under venerable and gigantic trees ... The villages were enchanting – opium dreams of delicate foliage and old white houses. Portsmouth is a city of the Georgian age – there is a glorious atavism to be derived from a ride through its shady residence streets.'

Sonia again visited New England on June 16. She was doing some business for her company at Magnolia, Massachusetts and dropped in on Providence. This time she met both aunts, getting on so well with them that she tried to persuade Annie to move to New York and share her apartment. Little did she know how Annie really felt about her. Lovecraft said, 'strange to say, my aunt likes her immensely despite a racial and social chasm which she doesn't often bridge.' Sonia's Jewishness and status as a working woman were anathema to Annie and her patrician Providence upbringing.

The Invisible Monster

Lovecraft spent a few days with Sonia in Gloucester and Magnolia during her time there in late June and early July. One evening, as they strolled along the esplanade in Magnolia with a full moon reflected in the sea, they heard a strange noise and Sonia suggested they had the makings of an 'interesting weird tale'. The result was 'The Horror at Martin's Beach' which she wrote and he revised but which was published in *Weird Tales* in November 1923 under her name only and titled 'The Invisible Monster'. It is a fairly improbable tale about a monster and hypnotism. There was, however, an extraordinary event the day following the couple's walk along the esplanade that Sonia later wrote about:

'His continued enthusiasm the next day was so genuine that in appreciation I surprised and shocked him right then and there by kissing him. He was so flustered that he blushed, then he turned pale. When I chaffed him about it he said he had not been kissed since he was a very small child and that he was never kissed by any women, not even his mother or aunts since he grew to manhood, and that he would probably never be kissed again. (But I fooled him.)'

It is quite extraordinary that Lovecraft claimed never to have been kissed since he was a child, surrounded by women as he was. It says quite a lot about how reserved his family was, to never have shown any sign of physical intimacy. Even for the time it is unusual and makes it perfectly understandable that Lovecraft found it difficult to know quite how to respond to this woman who seemed to be attracted to him.

Meanwhile, Sonia was nothing if not persistent. On Sunday, July 16, she was back in Rhode Island, traveling to Newport with Lovecraft and ten days later Lovecraft was back in Brooklyn, staying in her apartment on a three-day stopover during a trip to Cleveland to visit Galpin and Loveman. He remained there until August 15, talking non-stop.

He boasted to Aunt Lillian about how unconventional he had become: 'Can you picture me vestless, hatless, soft-collared, and belted, ambling about with a boy of twenty, as if I were no older?' It was doing him good, as he again wrote to Lillian: 'As for the kind of time I am having – it is simply great! I have just the incentive I need to keep me active & free from melancholy, & I look so well that I doubt if any Providence person would know me by sight! I have no headaches or depressed spells – in short, I am for the time being really alive & in good health & spirits. The companionship of youth & artistic taste is what keeps me going!'

A Growing Circle of Friends

It seemed that Lovecraft had finally discovered a normal existence and it was good for him. He was no longer under the smothering care of his mother and had finally broken away from Providence. He had broadened his mind and his aspirations with travel and had at last found real friends, people with whom he had much in common and who inspired him to do more. It must be remembered that he was, by now, 31 years old.

Around this time he met George Kirk (1898 – 1962) who was the publisher of Samuel Loveman's 1922 edition of Ambrose Bierce's *Twenty-One Letters*. He also met the poet Hart Crane (1899 – 1932) and was introduced into his circle of friends, men such as the Modernist painter, William Sommer (1867 – 1949) and the Swiss-American architect, William Lescaze (1896 – 1969). The little known composer Gordon Hatfield was part of Crane's group and was probably the first openly gay person that Lovecraft had ever encountered.

His response, when asked about Hatfield later was as could be expected: 'To be sure, I recall him! Dear, dear! How he used to sit cross-legged on the floor at Eglin's, little white sailor's cap tucked gracefully under one arm, sport shirt open at the neck, gazing soulfully up at Samuelus and discoursing of arts and harmonies of life! I'm afraid he thought me a very crude, stupid, commonplace, masculine sort of person.' He added on another occasion, 'I didn't know whether to kiss it or kill it!'

It is worthy of note that both Crane and Samuel Loveman were gay, but Lovecraft seems not to have let this stand in the way of his friendship with them, or perhaps he just did not realize their sexual orientation.

He traveled to New York on August 15, 1922 and remained there for two months, living in Sonia's apartment. His financial state was, as ever, parlous, but his friends were unstintingly generous towards him. In Cleveland, Galpin, Loveman and others paid for his meals and expenses while in New York he could rely on Frank Long and his parents to feed him and Sonia to help him in other ways. It demonstrates how fond people were of him. They wanted him to remain in their company in New York as long as possible.

Lovecraft in Brooklyn, 1922.

Visiting Hell's Kitchen

This New York visit was filled with sightseeing and Lovecraft made a couple of new acquaintances. Paul Livingstone Keil (1900 – 53) was a young amateur who published the magazine *Pauke's Quill*. He accompanied Lovecraft, Morton and Long on a visit to Edgar Allan Poe's cottage in Fordham. Keil would later write a memoir

of that day and became one of Lovecraft's numerous correspondents. He also met the children's author Everett McNeil (1862 – 1929). McNeil lived in the area of New York known as Hell's Kitchen on the west side of Manhattan. Lovecraft gives us a description of this notorious area of the city, managing to throw in some casual racism:

> 'Hell's Kitchen is the last remnant of the ancient slums – & by ancient I mean slums in which the denizens are not sly, cringing foreigners; but 'tough' and energetic members of the superior Nordic stock – Irish, German and American. The slinking Dago or Jew of the lower East Side is a strange, furtive animal ... he uses poison instead of fists, automatic revolvers instead of bricks and blackjacks. But west of Broadway the old toughs have made their last stand ... Squalor is extreme, but not so odorous as in the foreign districts. Churches flourish – for all the natives are devout & violent Roman Catholics. It was odd to see slums in which the denizens are Nordic – with shapely faces & often light hair & blue eyes.'

The Howling of Demons

One of Lovecraft's New York excursions resulted in a story – 'The Hound' – that he wrote when he returned to Providence in October. He and Kleiner visited the beautiful Dutch Reformed Church on Flatbush Avenue in Brooklyn which has an atmospheric old cemetery behind it. Lovecraft brought a bit of it back to Sonia's apartment. 'From one of the crumbling gravestones – dated 1747 – I chipped a small piece to carry away. It lies before me as I write – & ought to suggest some sort of a horror-story. I must some night place it beneath my pillow as I sleep ... who can say what *thing* might not come out of the centuried earth to exact vengeance for his desecrated tomb?'

'The Hound' was one of the five stories in Lovecraft's initial submission to *Weird Tales*, which he later dismissed as 'a dead dog' and 'a piece of junk'. It has not fared well

Hell's Kitchen, New York in the 1930s.

THE HOUND

The main characters in 'The Hound' are the narrator and his friend St John which was the nickname Lovecraft gave to Kleiner. These two men have a morbid interest in robbing graves, as the only way to escape the ennui from which they suffer. They keep their relics in a grim museum in the basement of their house and they really are grave-robbing experts, as the following passage demonstrates:

'The predatory excursions on which we collected our unmentionable treasures were always artistically memorable events. We were no vulgar ghouls, but worked only under certain conditions of mood, landscape, environment, weather, season, and moonlight. These pastimes were to us the most exquisite form of aesthetic expression, and we gave their details a fastidious technical care. An inappropriate hour, a jarring lighting effect, or a clumsy manipulation of the damp sod, would almost totally destroy for us that ecstatic titillation which followed the exhumation of some ominous, grinning secret of the earth.'

One day, they target the grave of a man in Holland who has been buried for five hundred years. This particular individual had also robbed graves and had 'stolen a potent thing from a mighty sepulchre'. On arriving at the cemetery they hear the distant baying of a hound but pay it no heed. They open the grave and discover an amulet that has engraved on it the 'oddly conventionalized figure of a crouching winged hound, or sphinx with a semi-canine face'. They take this object home with them to place in their basement museum. But, when they get home, there are strange goings-on. The house seems to be filled with whirring or flapping noises and the sound of 'faint, distant baying' can be heard across the moors.

One night, when walking home from the station, St John is attacked by 'some frightful carnivorous thing' and ripped to shreds. Dying, he gasps, 'The amulet – that damned thing.' The narrator now realizes that he must return the amulet to where they had found it but he is attacked and robbed of it one night in Rotterdam by a gang of thieves. Not long after, the city is horrified by a 'red death' in the thieves' den.

The narrator is somehow driven to return to the cemetery and dig up the grave where he finds the corpse within not as they had found it, 'not clean and placid as we had seen it then, but covered with caked blood and shreds of alien flesh and hair, and leering sentiently at me with phosphorescent sockets and sharp ensanguined fangs yawning twistedly in mockery of my inevitable doom.'

The narrator realizes that suicide is the only option left for him:

'Now, as the baying of that dead, fleshless monstrosity grows louder and louder, and the stealthy whirring and flapping of those accursed web-wings circles closer and closer, I shall seek with my revolver the oblivion which is my only refuge from the unnamed and unnamable.'

with critics either, several suggesting that its overblown prose must have been written with tongue in cheek, as some kind of self-parody. Its debt to Edgar Allan Poe has often been pointed out. 'Slavishly Poe-esque in style,' is how American science fiction and fantasy author, Lin Carter, described what he called 'a minor little tale'.

The story is notable for historians of the Cthulhu Mythos as it carries the first explicit mention of the *Necronomicon* and its compiler, Abdul Alhazred. Lovecraft writes of the amulet 'it was the thing hinted of in the forbidden *Necronomicon* of the mad Arab Abdul Alhazred'.

The word 'necronomicon' had come to Lovecraft in a dream. His attempt at a derivation suggests that *nekros* means corpse; *nomos* means law; and *eikon* means picture. The word, therefore, means 'An Image (or Picture) of the Law of the Dead'. Another interpretation suggests that it actually means 'A Consideration (or Classification) of the Dead'. The *Necronomicon* was, he later suggested, the Greek translation of a work in Arab entitled *Al Azif*. He had stolen this term from Samuel Henley's notes to William Beckford's Gothic masterpiece *Vathek*. He translates *azif* as 'a nocturnal sound ... believed to be the howling of demons.'

SEA ANEMONES (1904)
BY ERNST HAECKEL (1834 – 1919)

A German biologist, philosopher and artist, Haeckel's published artwork includes over 100 detailed, multi-color illustrations of animals and sea creatures. While Haeckel's art may have inspired some of Lovecraft's monsters, S.T. Joshi also cites Haeckel as one of Lovecraft's 'chief philosophical influences', especially in justifying his racist views. Haeckel had scientifically developed a ranking system for dividing up humans by levels of intelligence – Northern Europeans and Greeks were at the top with Africans and Australians at the bottom.

THE LURKING FEAR

The story begins melodramatically – 'There was a thunder in the air on the night I went to the deserted mansion atop Tempest Mountain to find the lurking fear'. The narrator, 'a connoisseur in horrors', takes two men to search for a mysterious being that has wreaked havoc amongst the squatters in the Catskills near the Martense mansion. They set up camp inside the deserted mansion but as a lightning storm approaches, they all mysteriously begin to feel drowsy and drift off to sleep on the same bed.

When the narrator awakes, his two companions – Bennett and Tobey – who were sleeping on either side of him have vanished, presumably taken by the monster. There is a flash of lightning and a monstrous shadow appears on the chimney:

> *Then came the devastating stroke of lightning which shook the whole mountain, lit the darkest crypts of the hoary grove, and splintered the patriarch of the twisted trees. In the demon flash of a monstrous fireball the sleeper started up suddenly while the glare from beyond the window threw his shadow vividly upon the chimney above the fireplace from which my eyes had never strayed. That I am still alive and sane, is a marvel I cannot fathom. I cannot fathom it, for the shadow on that chimney was not that of George Bennett or of any other human creature, but a blasphemous abnormality from hell's nethermost craters; a nameless, shapeless abomination which no mind could fully grasp and no pen even partly describe.'*

In the second installment, the narrator meets another journalist, Arthur Munroe, with whom he begins to investigate the lurking fear. They shelter from a thunderstorm in a house in a hamlet, aware that the creature is usually abroad in such weather. Munroe becomes fascinated by something outside and turns to look out the window. When the narrator tries to attract his attention and shakes the other man's shoulder, he discovers that Munroe is dead and his face has been eaten away.

In the third chapter, the narrator investigates the history of the Martense family, opening the grave of Jan Martense. This Dutch family, he learns, had been particularly reclusive and had hated the English, intermarrying with the people who worked on their estate. Jan Martense had tried to break out of this unhealthy lifestyle but had been killed because of it. The narrator digs down to his coffin and beyond, falling into a subterranean tunnel in which he sees two eyes reflecting his torch-beam in the distance. Managing to clamber up to the surface, he learns that the squatters have set fire to a cabin on the hillside, inside of which one of the monsters is trapped.

The concluding installment reveals the truth. There is more than one monster and these half-ape, half-mole creatures live in a honeycomb of passages in the hillside. They are the 'ultimate product of mammalian degeneration; the frightful outcome of isolated spawning, multiplication, and cannibal nutrition above and below the ground; the embodiment of the snarling chaos and grinning fear that lurk behind life.'

The narrator watches the creatures emerge from a hole and, under cover of a clap of thunder he shoots one of them as it struggles to keep up with the others. On examining it, he realizes it is, in fact, a member of the Martense family.

> *It had looked at me as it died, and its eyes had the same odd quality that marked those other eyes which had stared at me underground and excited cloudy recollections. One eye was blue, the other brown. They were the dissimilar Martense eyes of the old legends, and I knew in one inundating cataclysm of voiceless horror what had become of that vanished family; the terrible and thunder-crazed house of Martense.'*

Vol. II. No. 6

HOME BREW
MOONSHINE

AMERICA'S ZIPPIEST POCKET MA

Peppy Stories
Pungent Jests
Piquant Gossip

25¢

Edited
by
Missus and Mister
George Julian Houtain

MUTUAL
RESOLUTIONS

Begins In This Number
"The Lurking Fear"
By Howard P. Lovecraft
Illustrated by CLARK ASHTON SMITH the artist
Who Illustrated Edgar Allan Poe

Man's Revolt Against Marriage, By Winnifred Harper Cooley

Two very different looks for 'The Lurking Fear' – a 1994 movie poster and *Home Brew* magazine, 1923.

CLARK ASHTON SMITH

Lovecraft scholar, L. Sprague de Camp, said of Smith: '… nobody since Poe has so loved a well-rotted corpse'. He joined Lovecraft's circle of correspondents after the publication of his celebrated long poem in blank verse, *The Hashish Eater, or the Apocalypse of Evil* in *Ebony and Crystal* magazine solicited a fan letter from Lovecraft.

'I trust you will pardon the liberty taken by an absolute stranger in writing you, for I cannot refrain from expressing the appreciation aroused in me by your drawings & poetry, as shown me by my friend, Mr. Samuel Loveman, whom I am now visiting in Cleveland. Your book, containing matter only chronologically classifiable as juvenilia, impresses me as a work of the most distinguished genius.'

The two would remain friends until Lovecraft's death, frequently borrowing each other's fictional place names and the names of otherworldly gods for their stories. Like Lovecraft, Smith was inspired by nightmares he endured during sickness when he was young. Between 1929 and 1934, he wrote more than a hundred short stories, all in the genres of weird horror or science fiction.

The Horror in the Eyes

Lovecraft returned to Providence in mid-October 1922 and set to writing 'The Hound' but George Houtain was pursuing him for a second serial for *Home Brew* magazine. 'The Lurking Fear' was to be an improvement on his first effort. A four-part serialization, it had chapter titles imbued with dread – 'The Shadow on the Chimney', 'A Passer in the Storm', 'What the Red Glare Meant' and 'The Horror in the Eyes'. This time Lovecraft was spared the irksome task of providing a recap of what had gone before at the start of each new chapter. Houtain provided these. The story appeared in *Home Brew* from January to April 1923.

In 'The Lurking Fear', the theme of the evils of interbreeding is present. It would not be the last time it would crop up in Lovecraft's work. It had already appeared in 'Facts Concerning the Late Arthur Jermyn and His Family' and would do so in 'The Rats in the Walls' and *The Shadow Over Innsmouth*. Lovecraft's underlying message, unfortunately, is probably a racial one, a warning against breeding out of one's race or color.

The language of 'The Lurking Fear' is, quite simply, magnificent, but in places, it is so overblown that it comes dangerously close to parody. One passage towards the end of the story provides a perfect example:

'Shrieking, slithering, torrential shadows of red viscous madness chasing one another through endless, ensanguined corridors of purple fulgurous sky ... formless phantasms and kaleidoscopic mutations of a ghoulish, remembered scene; forests of monstrous overnourished oaks with serpent roots twisting and sucking unnamable juices from an earth verminous with millions of cannibal devils; mound-like tentacles groping from underground nuclei of polypous perversion ... insane lightning over malignant ivied walls and daemon arcades choking with fungous vegetation'

The serial was illustrated by Clark Ashton Smith who would become, along with Robert E. Howard and Lovecraft, one of the pre-eminent practitioners of weird fiction.

Epiphany in Marblehead

In mid-December 1922, Lovecraft braved the cold to visit Boston where he participated in a meeting of the Hub Club, a group of amateurs. He then spent time exploring Salem, a town that was made for Lovecraft with his fascination for the seventeenth century. He visited the Witch House, the House of the Seven Gables and other famous local historical sites. He took a bus up the coast to Marblehead and was overwhelmed by it. Seven years later, he was still enthusing about the beauty of the place when he first saw it.

'I account that instant – about 4:05 to 4:10 p.m., Dec. 17, 1922 – the most powerful single emotional climax experienced during my nearly forty years of existence. In a flash all the past of New England – all the past of Old England – all the past of Anglo-Saxondom and the Western World – swept over me and identified me with the stupendous totality of all things in such a way as it never did before and never will again. That was the high tide of my life.'

It would be a year before Lovecraft would introduce the impressions that he experienced that day and in many other New England explorations into his fiction with 'The Festival'. His 1920 story, 'The Picture in the House', had begun the journey but there was still some assimilation of the area's true nature, its history and antiquities and its people to be done before he created the work for which we know him best.

CHAPTER 6

THE RATS IN THE WALLS

A Question of Cash

Lovecraft had reduced his commitment to the UAPA, but suddenly, in November 1922, he was appointed interim President of its rival the National Amateur Press Association (NAPA). As Rheinhart Kleiner describes it, it was a momentous appointment. 'The amateur world rocked,' he wrote, 'when Lovecraft was announced as the new president. He formed an official board to replace a number of officials who had resigned when the former president had left his post and wrote the first of five official reports that would appear in the *National Amateur*.'

He pleaded for renewed amateur activity and put his money where his mouth was by promising to publish a second edition of his own magazine, *Conservative* that appeared in March 1923. He also published a third in July. By 1923, however, he was no longer president and had returned to the UAPA. He would have little involvement with the NAPA for the next ten years.

In late 1922, he was desperately short of cash and had to turn down an invitation from Samuel Loveman to go to Cleveland:

'De re Clevelandica – I wish to hell I could be more certain about the cash question! It looks like a damn gloomy season, for nerves & household illness have reduced my Bushic capacity to a minimum & I gotta helluva lotta expenses ahead ... So as I say, when I think of finance, my naturally long face tends to acquire an exaggeration of its original proportions! But still – if I can get me noives together enough to punish a record pile of Bush junk, there's no telling what I can do by July ... provided my conservative aunt doesn't make too big a kick against my barbaric extravagance.'

Those expenses of which he spoke included the printing of the *Conservative* and a new

suit which cost him $42 and which would be stolen from his apartment in Brooklyn two years later. The two issues of the *Conservative* he produced at this time featured many of his associates, including James Morton, Samuel Loveman, Alfred Galpin and Frank Belknap Long. The first of them, issue #12 of the magazine, was only eight pages long but the second consisted of twenty-eight pages. It includes Loveman's ode 'To Satan' which is dedicated to Lovecraft; 'Felis: A Prose Poem' by Long, a tribute to his cat; an essay and a prose poem by Galpin; a long poem in Scots dialect by Morton and writings by Lovecraft.

Return to Salem

In early 1923, Lovecraft visited the Salem-Marblehead area at least three times. His third trip in April first took him to Boston for a meeting of the Hub Club. Then he headed for Salem and Danvers – formerly known as Salem Village – where the 1692 witch trials had taken place. He visited the Samuel Fowler house, now a museum where he was greeted by 'two of the most pitiful and decrepit-looking persons imaginable – hideous old women more sinister than the witches of 1692 ...'. He reported that one of the women spoke to him 'in a hoarse rattling voice that dimly suggested death.'

He next made for the farmhouse built by Townsend Bishop in 1636, the house of Rebekah Nurse, accused of witchcraft by the slave Tituba and hanged on Gallows Hill. He was permitted by the caretaker to venture all the way up to the attic. Naturally, he milked the situation for all the horror he could in a description of it:

'Thick dust covered everything, & unnatural shapes loomed on every hand as the evening twilight oozed through the little

bleared panes of the ancient windows. I saw something hanging from the wormy ridge-pole – something that swayed as if in unison with the vesper breeze outside, though that breeze had no access to this funereal & forgotten place – shadows ... shadows ...'

The following day, he traveled to Merrimac and visited his young amateur acquaintance, Edgar J. Davis. They toured several graveyards and next day went to the coastal town of Newburyport and on April 16, Lovecraft set off for home. Marblehead was visited again in June and on July 2 – 3 he was in Boston for the Hub Club once again.

He met Sonia again in Providence between July 15 and 17, the first time they had seen each other since his New York sojourn of the previous September. It should be noted, however, that although they had not seen each other, Sonia later admitted that they were in correspondence virtually daily. Sometimes his letters to her extended to forty or fifty pages.

Sonia Greene, 1921

His Relentless Walking

In August, his friend Maurice W. Moe, with whom he had only corresponded, came to visit. The two took a bus to Boston where they met up with some other friends and Moe's wife and children. One of the friends described the day they spent with Lovecraft as relentless tour guide:

'I recall vividly the Saturday afternoon ... when Lovecraft, Moe, Albert Sandusky, and I went to Old Marblehead to visit the numerous Colonial houses and other places of interest with which Howard was thoroughly familiar. He was so insistent that our friend from the West should not miss a single relic or point of view over lovely town and harbor and walked us relentlessly for miles, impelled by his inexhaustible enthusiasm until our bodies rebelled and against his protests, we dragged ourselves to the train. Lovecraft was still buoyant.'

From this it is evident that Lovecraft was more robust, no longer the sickly invalid of

a few years previously. He emphasized this by undertaking a tour of Portsmouth, New Hampshire, after he had said goodbye to Moe and his family. He loved Portsmouth as a living city. 'For Portsmouth,' he wrote, 'is the one city which hath kept its own life and people as well as its houses and streets. There are scarce any inhabitants but the old families, and scarce any industries but the old ship-building and the navy yard which has been there since 1800.' He found there 'the living whirl of the real eighteenth century.' His more unsavory feelings are never far away though, because he notes the 'pure *English* faces' he sees in Portsmouth.

In September, James Morton arrived and they visited Marblehead and its environs. After Morton left, Lovecraft went home to bed, sleeping for twenty-one hours.

Writing for *Weird Tales*

Lovecraft always detested *Home Brew* magazine, describing it as a 'vile rag'. It must have been very good news, therefore, when he heard of a new magazine called *Weird Tales*. It would be the first publication devoted purely to fiction of the type in which Lovecraft was interested. None had existed even back in the day of Poe who had published his stories in the general periodicals of his time such as *Graham's Magazine, Godey's Lady's Book* and *Southern Literary Messenger.*

Ambrose Bierce, another writer of the strange and weird had been published widely in magazines and newspapers. Munsey's magazines, launched in the 1890s, published a great deal of weird fiction as well as detective stories and speculative fiction. But in the 1920s, the genres began to become somewhat ghettoized. In fact, 'weird' did not exist really as a genre at the start of the twentieth century and for some time after, and H.P. Lovecraft may have been the first writer to consider himself mainly a writer of 'weird fiction'. Therefore, *Weird Tales* must have seemed like a breath of fresh air.

Weird, Macabre and Fantastic Stories

Liking what he saw in the first few issues of *Weird Tales,* Lovecraft sent some stories off to its editor, Edwin Baird. Unfortunately, his cover letter was a disaster. Sprague de Camp observed that in the letter 'Lovecraft had done everything to assure rejection of his stories ... He all but begged Baird to return his manuscripts.' The arrogance and superior air of his opening paragraph was enough to put anyone off.

'My Dear Sir
Having a habit of writing weird, macabre and fantastic stories for my own amusement, I have lately been simultaneously hounded by nearly a dozen well-meaning friends into deciding to submit a few of these Gothic horrors to your newly founded periodical ... I have no idea if these things will be found suitable, for I pay no attention to the demands of commercial writing ... the only reader I hold in mind is myself. ... I like *Weird Tales* very much, though I have seen only the April number. Most of the stories, of course, are more or less commercial – or should I say conventional? – in technique, but they all have an enjoyable angle.'

Baird wrote at the end of this letter: 'Despite the foregoing, or because of it, we are using some of Mr Lovecraft's unusual stories'. They appeared between October 1923 and February 1926, for a payment of 1.5 cents per word. Lovecraft was very irritated by Baird's habit of giving the stories he published new titles without consulting with their author. Therefore, 'Facts Concerning the Late Arthur Jermyn and His Family' appeared as 'The White Ape'. Lovecraft angrily retorted, 'you may be sure that if I ever titled a story "The White Ape", there would be no ape in it!' But, he was secretly delighted to have his stories accepted by a proper professional magazine such as *Weird Tales* and it spurred him on to write three new stories in the autumn of 1923, within a few weeks of each other – 'The Rats in the Walls', 'The Unnamable' and 'The Festival'.

'The Rats in the Walls' arose from what Lovecraft called 'a very commonplace incident – the cracking of wall-paper late at night and the chain of imaginings resulting from it.' In his commonplace book there is another source for the germination of the story – 'Horrible secret in crypt of ancient castle – discovered by dweller.' A phrase in Poe's 'The Fall of the House of Usher' may also have been part of the inspiration for the story. Sir Roderick Usher claims that his hearing is so sensitive that he 'can hear the rats in the walls.' The plot is deceptively simple.

A Thousand Shapes of Horror

J.C. Henneberger loved 'The Rats in the Walls', describing it as the best that *Weird Tales* had received to-date. Little did he know, it had already been rejected by *Argosy All-Story Weekly.*

Lovecraft's second story of that autumn brought back his character, Randolph Carter. He described him as an unsuccessful author who, like Lovecraft, was prone to faint when stressed, hardly conducive to going up against hideous monsters and demonic fiends. The story was 'The Unnamable'.

WEIRD TALES

Weird Tales was launched as a monthly magazine in Chicago by J.C. Henneberger, a former journalist. The first editor was Edwin Baird, assisted by Farnsworth Wright. As well as Lovecraft, it published C.M. Eddy Jr, Clark Ashton Smith and Seabury Quinn, writer of the very popular Jules de Grandin stories. The magazine was losing money under Baird's stewardship – he ran up debts amounting to $40,000 and after thirteen issues he was fired.

Lovecraft was offered the job as editor but turned it down, claiming that he did not want to re-locate to Chicago, leaving his beloved Providence. '… think of the tragedy of such a move for an aged librarian,' he wrote to his friend Frank Long. The fact that he was only 34 and far from aged, did not seem to matter. The job went, instead to Baird's assistant, Farnsworth Wright who would remain in that role for fifteen years and 179 issues.

Lovecraft would find Wright more picky than Baird and the editor famously rejected a number of his stories including *At the Mountains of Madness, The Shadow Over Innsmouth* and, to begin with, 'The Call of Cthulhu'. On the other hand, he discovered writers such as Robert Bloch and Robert E. Howard.

Wright died in 1940 and the magazine declined in popularity until it ceased publication in September 1954, after publishing 279 editions. It has been revived several times in the subsequent decades and is now owned by Viacom/MTV who are rumored to have a television series in mind although this has not been confirmed.

New—never-before published novel **by LOVECRAFT**

"Last of the Lovecrafts"—Says Its Discoverer, August W. Derleth

MAY

Weird Tales

15¢

Cover of *Weird Tales*, May 1941, in which *The Case of Charles Dexter Ward* appeared. Cover art by Hannes Bok.

A montage of *Weird Tales* classic covers.

THE RATS IN THE WALLS

The story is set in 1923 and is narrated by a Virginian named Delapore (formerly de la Poer) who has relocated to Exham Priory, his family's ancestral estate in England from Massachusetts. His ancestor had fled to Virginia after a catastrophe had befallen his entire family for which he had been blamed. Delapore begins to restore the priory, much to the dismay of the locals, especially as he shows himself to be ignorant of the history of the place. He moves in but now and then hears rats scurrying behind the walls. His cats, in particular his favorite, Nigger Man (the name of Lovecraft's cat when he was a child), also hear the noises.

Delapore learns from bad dreams and further investigation that his ancestors had created an underground city centuries previously and that they ate human flesh. They raised 'human cattle' for generations, some of whom had regressed to walking on all-fours. Driven insane by this knowledge,

and tapping into feelings passed down through the centuries, Delapore attacks a friend in the vast underground city and begins eating him. He is caught and sent to an asylum. Not long after, Exham Priory is destroyed. Delapore maintains his innocence, declaring that it had not been him who had eaten his friend. It was the rats in the walls:

'They are trying, too, to suppress most of the facts concerning the priory. When I speak of poor Norrys they accuse me of this hideous thing, but they must know that I did not do it. They must know it was the rats; the slithering, scurrying rats whose scampering will never let me sleep; the daemon rats that race behind the padding in this room and beckon me down to greater horrors than I have ever known; the rats they can never hear; the rats, the rats in the walls.'

'The Rats in the Walls', *Weird Tales*, March 1924. Illustration by William F. Heitman.

It is a story filled with the type of New England horror that became typical of Lovecraft's work. '... no wonder sensitive students shudder at the Puritan age in Massachusetts. So little is known of what went on beneath the surface – so little, yet such a ghastly festering as it bubbles up putrescently in occasional ghoulish glimpses.'

There is also an element of self-deprecation. Manton criticizes Carter at one point for his fascination with things that are

'unmentionable' or 'unnamable', describing this as 'a very puerile device, quite in keeping with my lowly standing as an author. I was too fond of ending my stories with sights or sounds which paralyzed my heroes' faculties and left them without courage, words, or associations to tell what they had experienced.' These were probably things of which Lovecraft had been accused in his writing.

THE UNNAMABLE

Carter is in New England where he meets his close friend, Joel Manton (based upon Lovecraft's friend, Maurice W. Moe) in an 'old burying ground' near a ruined house on Meadow Hill in the fictional town of Arkham, Massachusetts. Seated on a seventeenth century tomb, Carter tells his friend about a being that is said to haunt the house and its environs. This creature cannot be seen or described and is, therefore known as the 'unnamable'. They discuss the unknown throughout the afternoon, Manton berating his companion for his belief in the supernatural. Suddenly, however, at the end of the day, they are attacked by an unknown creature:

'Then came a noxious rush of noisome, frigid air from that same dreaded direction, followed by a piercing shriek just beside me on that shocking rifted tomb of man and monster. In another instant I was knocked from my gruesome bench by the devilish threshing of some unseen entity of titanic size but undetermined nature; knocked sprawling on the root-clutched mold of that abhorrent graveyard, while from the tomb came such a stifled uproar of gasping and whirring that my fancy peopled the rayless gloom with Miltonic legions of the misshapen damned. There was a vortex of withering, ice-cold wind, and then the rattle of loose bricks and plaster; but I had mercifully fainted before I could learn what it meant.'

Carter and Manton awake in St. Mary's Hospital, scarred and bruised by what seem to have been horns and hooves. When Carter asks his friend what had attacked them, he replies chillingly, ' No – it wasn't that way at all. It was everywhere – a gelatin – a slime yet it had shapes, a thousand shapes of horror beyond all memory. There were eyes – and a blemish. It was the pit – the maelstrom – the ultimate abomination. Carter, it was the unnamable !'

Where Supernatural Forces Gather

The final story of the autumn, 'The Festival', is generally, regarded as the first story set in the Cthulhu Mythos and is something of a 3,000-word prose poem. It is set in the fictional town of Kingsport which was modeled on the town of Marblehead that had made a staggering impression on Lovecraft when he had visited it in December 1922.

Lovecraft revealed the source of this very original story. 'In intimating an alien race I had in mind the survival of pre-Aryan sorcerers who preserved primitive rites like those of the witch-cult – I had been reading Miss Murray's *The Witch Cult in Western Europe*.' In her landmark work, the revered English anthropologist and folklorist, Margaret Murray, had championed the notion – now discredited – that witchcraft had originated with a pre-Aryan race that had been driven underground and still inhabited remote parts of the earth. Furthermore, Lovecraft had been reading something similar in stories by the Welsh author, Arthur Machen (1863 – 1947).

'The Festival' however, was an important story, making Arkham for the first time a place where supernatural forces gathered. In the story, time is defeated, past and present seeming to exist simultaneously, as they did when Lovecraft first gazed upon Marblehead/Kingsport.

The sense of place is overwhelming in the story, something that permeates the best of Lovecraft's work. His descriptions of the town and its streets and buildings evoke an atmosphere of deep foreboding. Lovecraft was reluctant to travel far beyond the outskirts of Providence but he visited New England's historical towns and villages searching for the past and escaping from the trappings of modernity that he feared would engulf the United States.

THE FESTIVAL

This story is set against the backdrop of Christmas, but the narrator of the story reminds us in ringing alliteration that Christmas is merely the continuation of a much older celebration, 'older than Bethlehem and Babylon, older than Memphis and mankind.' He arrives in Kingsport for the first time and it seems to him ancient and uninhabited. He finds the house of his relatives where he is greeted by a wordless old man with 'flabby hands, curiously gloved.'

The narrator suspects that the old man's 'bland face' is, in fact, a 'fiendishly cunning mask'. He is seated next to a pile of books amongst which is a Latin translation of the *Necronomicon*, 'of the mad Arab Abdul Alhazred, in Olaus Wormius' forbidden Latin translation; a book which I had never seen, but of which I had heard monstrous things whispered.' He reads it and discovers 'a thought and a legend too hideous for sanity or consciousness.' At eleven o'clock, he is led out of the house by the still silent old man to join a crowd of cloaked figures who emerge from the doorways of Kingsport.

They walk silently towards a white church on top of a hill in the center of town where they enter a secret passage beneath the crypt. They arrive at 'a vast fungous shore litten by a belching column of sick greenish flame and washed by a wide oily river that flowed from abysses frightful and unsuspected to join the blackest gulfs of immemorial ocean.' They engage in a rite, but the narrator becomes aware of creatures in the space:

Out of the unimaginable blackness beyond the gangrenous glare of that cold flame, out of the Tartarean leagues through which that oily river rolled uncanny, unheard, and unsuspected, there flopped rhythmically a horde of tame, trained, hybrid winged things that no sound eye could ever wholly grasp, or sound brain ever wholly remember. They were not altogether crows, nor moles, nor buzzards, nor ants, nor vampire bats, nor decomposed human beings; but something I cannot and must not recall. They flopped limply

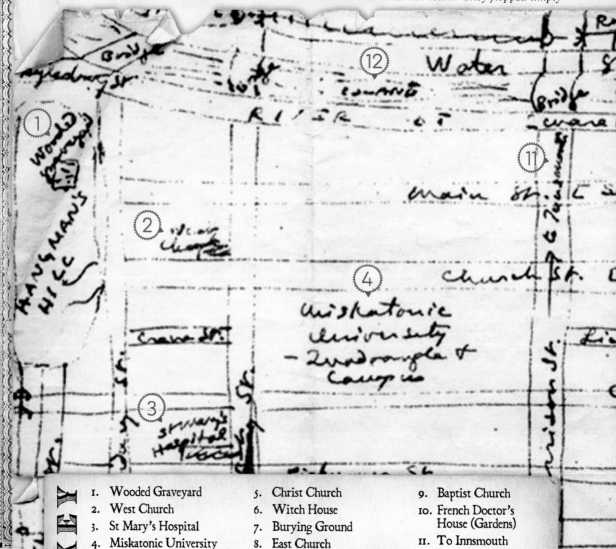

along, half with their webbed feet and half with their membraneous wings; and as they reached the throng of celebrants the cowled figures seized and mounted them, and rode off one by one along the reaches of that unlighted river, into pits and galleries of panic where poison springs feed frightful and undiscoverable cataracts.

The old man points out to the narrator the family resemblance that can be discerned in their faces, but he refuses to join the others in mounting one of the creatures and flying off. The old man shows him a watch bearing his family's coat of arms that he knows was buried with his great-great-great-great grandfather in 1698.

Suddenly the wax mask is dislodged from the old man's face and the narrator launches himself into the underground river, 'into that putrescent juice of earth's inner horrors before the madness of my screams could bring down upon me all the charnel legions these pest-gulfs might conceal.' He wakes up in hospital in Kingsport, having been told that he had walked off a cliff. He is transferred to St. Mary's Hospital in Arkham where he obtains a copy of the *Necronomicon*. He finds the passage that had so disturbed him at the old man's house and realizes that he has, in fact read it before:

> 'The nethermost caverns,' wrote the mad Arab, 'are not for the fathoming of eyes that see; for their marvels are strange and terrific. Cursed the ground where dead thoughts live new and oddly bodied, and evil the mind that is held by no head. Wisely did Ibn Schacabao say, that happy is the tomb where no wizard hath lain, and happy the town at night whose wizards are all ashes. For it is of old rumor that the soul of the devil-bought hastes not from his charnel clay, but fats and instructs the very worm that gnaws; till out of corruption horrid life springs, and the dull scavengers of earth wax crafty to vex it and swell monstrous to plague it. Great holes secretly are digged where earth's pores ought to suffice, and things have learnt to walk that ought to crawl.'

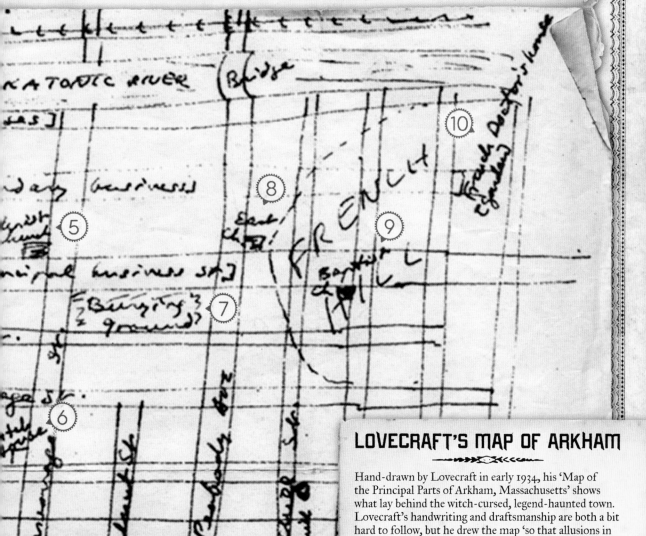

LOVECRAFT'S MAP OF ARKHAM

Hand-drawn by Lovecraft in early 1934, his 'Map of the Principal Parts of Arkham, Massachusetts' shows what lay behind the witch-cursed, legend-haunted town. Lovecraft's handwriting and draftsmanship are both a bit hard to follow, but he drew the map 'so that allusions in any future tale I may write may be consistent.' (See key for clarification.)

ARTHUR MACHEN

Lovecraft discovered the work of Arthur Machen in summer 1923. Machen's best work had been done in the 1890s and by the time Lovecraft found him he was declining in reputation. Descended from a long line of clergymen, he had been born Arthur Llewelyn Jones in Caerleon, Monmouthshire in Wales in 1863. Around 1890, Machen's work began to be published in literary magazines, his stories influenced by Robert Louis Stevenson and using gothic and fantastic themes.

His first success was 'The Great God Pan' published in 1894. The story was a scandal, denounced for its sexual and horror content. Nonetheless, it sold very well and was re-printed. A novel, *The Three Imposters* followed in 1895 but the scandal involving Oscar Wilde later that year made it difficult for works of decadent horror such as Machen's to find a publisher. Some of his best work, therefore, was published later.

The death of his wife in 1899 devastated him and it took him some time to recover. His recovery was helped, however, by a career change. In 1901 he became an actor, a member of Frank Benson's company of traveling players. He re-married in 1903 and in 1906 his literary career began to flourish once more with a collection of his unpublished work of the previous decade. He continued to mix acting with journalism but money was tight.

His journalism during the First World War brought him once again to prominence when he published 'The Bowmen' which was the cause of the Angels of Mons incident on the Western Front. He capitalized on this publicity, publishing a series of morale-boosting stories.

In 1922 some of his older work was published and began to sell both in Britain and in America. But by 1926, the sudden interest in him had waned and once again he was facing financial hardship.

He died in 1947, aged 84. Lovecraft described Machen as the 'greatest living author' and read as much of his writings as he could get his hands on, but it was the Welsh writer's horror stories that he really enjoyed.

C.M. EDDY JR

Lovecraft, it turned out, was not the only writer of weird fiction in Providence. Clifford Martin Eddy Jr (1896 – 1967) had been born in Providence and lived with his wife Muriel in the eastern part of town, three miles from Lovecraft. He had published his first story, 'Sign of the Dragon', a detective story, in *Mystery Magazine* in 1919. Ghost and mystery stories followed. He and Lovecraft met in August 1923 from which time Lovecraft became a frequent visitor at the Eddys' house and Eddy and his wife were amongst those who persuaded Lovecraft to submit work to *Weird Tales*.

Lovecraft edited and revised a number of Eddy's stories, although occasionally the revision involved a total re-write. In return, in lieu of a fee the Eddys would type out his manuscripts for him. Lovecraft hated typing. Muriel Eddy described Lovecraft's physical exhaustion during a trip they all made together. 'Mr. Eddy almost had to carry Lovecraft back from the rural excursion, at least a mile, to the trolley line, for, unaccustomed to such vigorous jaunts at that time, the writer of tales macabre soon became so exhausted he could hardly move one foot after the other.'

Lovecraft enjoyed Eddy's company as he explained in a letter to Edwin Baird towards the end of 1923. 'I find Eddy rather a delight – I wish I had known him before.' Eddy was not of the intellectual caliber of Lovecraft, but it seems that Lovecraft was delighted to find someone with similar interests in his hometown.

PART 3
THE CALL
OF CTHULHU

CHAPTER 7

A MARRIED MAN

A Change of Circumstances

In a memoir Frank Belknap Long wrote in 1975, he talked of his first meeting with Lovecraft, in Sonia Greene's New York apartment in April 1922:

> 'It was at this point that something which at first had been a mere suspicion began to lodge itself more firmly in my mind. During the brief talk by the window, Howard had dwelt at some length on Sonia's meeting with his aunts and on two other occasions when they had spent considerable time together on New England terrain, with the Boston convention several weeks in the past. Could it be possible – it was possible, of course ... his relationship with Sonia had taken on what could only be thought of as a just-short-of-engagement character. It still was only at the friendship stage perhaps, but with the distinct possibility that it might soon become something more.'

Despite Long's suspicion, possibly arrived at with a degree of hindsight, the marriage of Howard Phillips Lovecraft to Sonia Haft Greene surprised and even shocked many of their friends. Rheinhart Kleiner's reaction was probably fairly typical. 'I do remember very well,' he wrote, 'That it was while riding in a taxi with Mr. and Mrs. Houtain ... that the news of the Lovecraft-Greene marriage was imparted to me. At once I had a feeling of sickness at the pit of my stomach and became very pale. Houtain laughed uproariously at the effect of his announcement, but agreed that he felt as I did.'

The Eddys were similarly taken aback by the news. C.M. Eddy Jr wrote: 'The next news we had of Lovecraft was an engraved announcement of his marriage to Sonia Greene. It was a simple announcement, but it took us so completely by surprise that it was

several hours before we thoroughly digested the news.' The announcement read:

Howard Phillips Lovecraft
And
Sonia Haft Greene

Announce their marriage
On Monday the third of March
One thousand nine hundred
and twenty-four.

Mr. and Mrs. Howard Phillips Lovecraft
At Home on and after March thirtieth, 1924
259 Parkside Avenue
Brooklyn, New York

A Permanent Literary Position

It took Lovecraft six days after the wedding to write to his Aunt Lillian to inform her of his changed circumstances. He had simply got on the 11.09 train from Providence to New York on Sunday, March 2, 1924 and next day had married Sonia. He had even written postcards to his aunts in the two days after the wedding but failed to mention it. He may have made them suspect something was afoot, however, when in one of his postcards on those two days he spoke of a 'permanent literary position' that he might get.

When he did finally write to tell them, he explained why the pair had decided to tie the knot, but goes about it in his customarily long-winded manner:

> '... it began to become apparent that I was not alone in finding psychological solitude more or less of a handicap. A detailed intellectual and aesthetic acquaintance since 1921, and a three-months visit in 1922 wherein congeniality was tested and found perfect in an infinity of ways, furnished abundant proof not only that S.H.G. is the most inspiriting and encouraging influence

Rheinhart Kleiner, Sonia Greene and Lovecraft in Boston, 1921.

which could possibly be brought to bear on me, but that she herself had begun to find me more congenial than anyone else, and had come to depend to a great extent on my correspondence and conversation for mental contentment and artistic and philosophical enjoyment.'

As ever, Lovecraft proves himself incapable of talking about his feelings and especially love. He presents his relationship with Sonia as an intellectual one, based on 'mental contentment' and 'artistic and philosophical enjoyment'. There is no doubt that Lovecraft was a virgin when he married Sonia. He had enjoyed no romantic liaisons when he was younger or in the years since.

Fingers Intertwining

Apparently, he had read several books on the subject of sex before his marriage and, although he was never the one to initiate any sexual contact with his wife, when she did, he always responded, she later said. It is probable that he was quite simply a man with a low sex drive. Sonia said that 'As a married man he was an adequately excellent lover, but refused to show his feelings in the presence of others. He shunned promiscuous association with women before his marriage.'

He would apparently express his feelings for Sonia by intertwining his little finger with hers and utter 'Umph!' On his feelings of love for her, she said:

'I believe he loved me as much as it was possible for a temperament like his to love. He'd never mention the word love. He would say instead, "My dear, you don't know how much I appreciate you." I tried to understand him and was grateful for any crumbs from his lips that fell my way.'

In the letter he justifies not inviting his aunts to the wedding ceremony or even discussing it beforehand, citing his 'hatred of sentimental spoofing' and the 'agonizingly indecisive talking over' that such events produce. This would seem to suggest that perhaps he had been afraid that Lillian and Annie would not approve of the idea of him marrying Sonia and would have tried to talk him out of it had they known beforehand. They were still wary of Sonia's foreignness and her status as a businesswoman. Perhaps they would also be reluctant to see Lovecraft leave home and even move away from Providence.

Proposing A Life Together

Moving away had seemed to Lovecraft inevitable in the months and weeks preceding the marriage. Perhaps he and Sonia had already made the decision, but he wrote to Clark Ashton Smith five weeks before the wedding, saying, 'Like you, I don't know anyone who is at all congenial here; & I believe I shall migrate to New York in the end – perhaps when Loveman does.'

Then to Edwin Baird a month before the marriage, he wrote that 'finances will decree a final disintegration [of the household in Providence] landing me in all probability in New York'. Sonia later said, 'I well knew that he was not in a position to marry, yet his letters indicated his desire to leave his home town and settle in New York.'

She was much more open about the marriage:

Exchange Place, Providence, RI in the 1920s.
Today, Exchange Place is known as Kennedy Plaza.

We each meditated and re-meditated upon the possibilities of a life together. Some of our friends suspected that we cared for one another, and upon friendly inquiry I admitted that I cared very much, that I took everything into consideration and decided that if he would have me I'd gladly be his wife. But nothing definitely had been said to anyone ... During our few years of correspondence and the many business trips I took to New England I did not fail to mention many of the adverse circumstances that were likely to ensue, but that we would have to work out these problems between us, and if we really cared more for one another than for the problems that might stand in our way, there was no reason why our marriage should not be a success. He thoroughly agreed ... Before leaving Providence for N.Y. I requested him to tell his aunts that he was going to marry me but he said he preferred to surprise them. In the matter of securing a marriage license, buying the ring and other details incumbent upon a marriage, he seemed so jovial. He said one would think that he was being married for the nth time, he went about it in such a methodical way.'

Hitting the Matrimonial Ties

As for the Anglican wedding ceremony itself, Lovecraft had a ball, it seems, as he described in a letter to James Morton:

'Yes, my boy, you got it the first time. Eager to put Colonial architecture to all of its possible uses, I hit the ties hither last week; and on Monday, March the Third, seized by the hair of the head of the President of the United – S.H.G. – and dragged her to Saint Paul's Chapel ... where after considerable assorted genuflection, and with the aid of the honest curate, Father George Benson Cox, and of two less ecclesiastical hangers-on, I succeeded in affixing to her series of patronymics the not unpretentious one of Lovecraft. Damned quaint of me, is it not? You never can tell what a guy like me is gonna do next!'

Asked in interviews many years later why Lovecraft had married Sonia, Samuel Loveman suggested that he had done it because of her interest in his work and her encouragement of his efforts. Because of this, he felt obliged to marry her. Frank Belknap Long, however, claimed that Lovecraft married Sonia because it was the proper thing for a gentleman to take a wife. At any rate, Lovecraft found it all very amusing, taking delight in referring to Sonia in the coming weeks as 'the wife' or 'the missus'.

Cosmopolitan and Contemporary

One can only speculate about Lovecraft's feelings for Sonia. She had come into his life in the weeks after his mother's passing. Was she, therefore, no more than a replacement for Susie? Another strong woman who could exercise control over his life? Perhaps, but Sonia was very different to Susie. She was emotionally open unlike Lovecraft's closed and restrained mother. She was cosmopolitan and contemporary and she earned her living, a notion that was anathema to Susie's Victorian mores.

It is certainly true that it was Sonia who pursued him. She mentioned 'the many business trips I took to New England' and she certainly visited him a great deal more than he visited her in New York. His letters to her would have revealed a lot about how he actually felt about Sonia, but unfortunately she took them into a field after their divorce in 1926 and burned them.

Nonetheless, they were married and life was hectic. Lovecraft was engaged on a strange ghostwriting job. It was to write a story for the great escape artist, Harry Houdini (1874 – 1926), to be published in *Weird Tales*. When he discovered that there was not a shred of truth to the story, he asked the *Weird Tales* owner, J.C. Henneberger, to let him embellish it. He finished it at the end of February 1924, but lost the manuscript on March 2, in Union Station in Providence when taking the train to New York the day before his wedding. Fortunately, he had another copy and on the morning of his wedding, he was furiously re-typing it. He had only typed half of it when it was time to head for the church.

Honey-Moon with Houdini

The plan had been to go to Philadelphia after the wedding, but Lovecraft and Sonia were too tired and returned to her apartment. Of course, there was still the Houdini manuscript to be finished. On arriving in Philadelphia the following day, Sonia read out from the copy while Lovecraft banged away on a borrowed typewriter. That was how they spend the first day and a half of their married life. 'When that manuscript was finished,' she wrote, 'we were too tired and exhausted for honey-mooning or anything else.' The story was sent off and later that month Lovecraft was paid $100 for it, the most money he had earned to-date for a story.

Editor at Large

In the issue of *Weird Tales* in which this story appeared, Lovecraft looms large, with his story 'Hypnos' and C.M. Eddy's 'The Loved Dead' that he had worked on. In fact, the latter story caused this issue of the magazine to be banned because Eddy's tale was about necrophilia and was in breach of obscenity regulations.

Weird Tales was becoming important to Lovecraft and Henneberger had told him he wanted him to become editor of his magazine. Edwin Baird had been ousted from his position as editor and Farnsworth Wright was acting editor. However, this would entail Lovecraft re-locating to Chicago. Sonia was in favour of him accepting the offer even though it would mean that she would either have to give up her job and move with him or they would have to live apart.

But Lovecraft may have been aware of the perilous state of Henneberger's finances at the time. He had lost more than $50,000 on *Weird Tales* and *Detective Tales*. Lovecraft declined the offer and perhaps it was a wise decision. It is doubtful, anyway, whether he would have made a good editor of a pulp magazine such as *Weird Tales*. With his high literary standards, he would have rejected a good deal of what was normally published in the magazine.

In the end, Henneberger sold *Detective Tales* and installed Farnsworth Wright as editor of *Weird Tales*, a position he would retain until 1940. Lovecraft would have a fractious relationship with Wright who rejected some of his best work, including *At the Mountains of Madness* and *The Shadow Over Innsmouth*. Lovecraft was not alone. Wright also rejected Robert E. Howard's 'The Frost Giant's Daughter' and Clark Ashton Smith's 'The Seven Geases', both important works in those authors' oeuvres. In reality, however, it could be argued in Wright's defense that he was merely doing his job, giving his readers what they wanted and if that meant a host of bad fiction, then so be it.

Married Life

In February 1924 Sonia lost her $10,000 a year job at Ferle Heller's. She did, fortunately, have substantial savings that gave her some time to find a new job. Lovecraft, meanwhile, applied for jobs at magazines, a literary agency and even took on a job as a salesman with a bill-collecting agency in Newark, New Jersey. He would have responsibilities for not actually collecting outstanding monies, but for selling the services of the agency. Employed on a trial basis, he lasted less than a week. The head of the Newark branch of the business was nothing if not honest with Lovecraft:

'... my guide became very candid about the tone of the business, and admitted that a gentleman born and bred has very little chance for success in such lines of canvassing salesmanship ... where one must be miraculously magnetic and captivating,

HARRY HOUDINI
IMPRISONED WITH THE PHARAOHS

'Imprisoned with the Pharaohs' is narrated by Houdini in the first person. In Egypt in January 1910, he has enlisted the services of a guide named Abdul Reis el Drogman. While on a tour of Cairo, Houdini has to break up a fight between his guide and a Bedouin leader, Ali Ziz. Drogman suggests that the quarrel be settled by a boxing match on top of the Great Pyramid of Giza. It transpires, however, that the fight was no more than a trick to get Houdini into the desert at night and kidnap him.

He is overpowered, bound and gagged and dropped down a deep pit. Houdini experiences strange dreams but when he awakes, succeeds in undoing the ropes that bind him. He suspects that he is somewhere under the Great Sphinx of Giza and, in the dark, starts to make his way through the labyrinthine passages, following what he believes to be a draft of air.

He discovers to his horror, however, that he has actually been traveling further underground. In the dark, he falls down a flight of stairs and finds himself in a large ceremonial cavern where he sees an army of half-man, half-animal mummies, at the head of which are the pharaohs Khephren and Nitokris.

They are making offerings to a huge, five-headed creature with tentacles that has appeared from a hole in the hall. Escaping this terrifying sight, Houdini realizes that this creature is merely the paw of the massive deity in whose image the Sphinx was carved. He dismisses what he saw as a dream or hallucination, but realizes that Khephren and his guide Drogman look very much alike.

'That extreme descent is too vivid a memory to be dismissed – and it is odd that no one has ever been able to find a man answering the description of my guide, Abdul Reis el Drogman – the tomb-throated guide who looked and smiled like King Khephren.'

Escape artist, Harry Houdini, in chains.

or else so boorish and callous that he can transcend every rule of tasteful conduct and push conversation on bored hostile, and unwilling victims.'

Definitely Marketable Attributes

One of the reasons he never found a position might be attributed to his arrogance and pomposity. He sent a letter to the *New York Times*, the *Herald Tribune* and other newspapers looking for work and telling them that they should ignore the fact that he has no experience. It is little wonder he did not find employment. 'The case is one,' he wrote, 'wherein certain definitely marketable attributes must be put forward in an unconventional manner if they are to override the current fetish which demands commercial experience and causes prospective employers to dismiss unheard the application of any situation-seeker unable to boast of a specific professional service in a given line.'

That approach having failed, he began to advertise his services in the *New York Times* classified section. Needless to say, it was unsuccessful:

WRITER AND REVISER, free-lance, desires regular and permanent salaried connection with any responsible enterprise requiring literary services; exceptionally thorough experience in preparing correct and fluent text on subjects assigned, and in meeting the most difficult, intricate and extensive problems of rewriting and constructive revision, prose or verse; would also consider situation dealing with such proofreading as demands rapid and discriminating perception, orthographical accuracy, stylish fastidiousness and a keenly developed sense of the niceties of English usage; good typist; age 34, married; has for seven years handled all the prose and verse of a leading American public speaker and editor. Y 2392 Times Annex.

Some Drastic Decisions

Then Sonia was taken ill with a gastric complaint that necessitated an eleven-day stay in Brooklyn Hospital and a long period of recuperation in the quiet of the countryside. While she was in hospital, he visited her every day which is a little surprising as he never once set foot inside the Butler Hospital when his mother was there.

Meanwhile, he was out with his friends a great deal and, in fact, had spent little time with his wife in September/October. On November 10, the day after he accompanied Sonia to the rest home in Somerville, New Jersey to recuperate after her illness, he was off on his travels again, traveling to Philadelphia to peruse its colonial antiquities, and staying at the YMCA.

On her return, they made some drastic decisions. Firstly, they would economize, but secondly, she would accept the offer of a job in a department store in Cincinnati and Lovecraft would move into a smaller apartment. Sonia later wrote:

'After we were married and I found it necessary to accept an exceedingly poor remunerative position out of town I suggested he have one of his friends live with him at our apartment, but his aunts thought it best that since I would be in town only a few days every three or four weeks when I'd come to town on a purchasing tour for my firm, it would be wiser to store most of my things and find a studio room large enough for Howard's book-cases and furniture that he brought with him from Providence.'

There appears to be a note of anger in this that it was her things that should go into storage. In fact, items of her furniture, including her piano, were sold off. Other items, including her books were sold, but it was said that Lovecraft held on to his stuff with 'tenacity'. 'I must have the Dr. Clark table and chair,' he wrote, 'the typewriter table & chair, the cabinet, the 454 library table, & several bookcases – to say nothing of some sort of bed or couch, & a bureau or chiffonier.'

Entirely Too Stylish

Lovecraft had always been thin, although in 1922 to 1923 he had put on weight. When they married, he had become thin again. Sonia later wrote:

> *When we were married he was tall and gaunt and 'hungry-looking'. I happen to like the apparently ascetic type but H.P. was too much even for my taste, so I used to cook a well-balanced meal every evening, make a substantial breakfast (he loved cheese soufflé! – rather an untimely dish for breakfast) and I'd leave a few (almost Dagwoodian) sandwiches for him, a piece of cake and some fruit for his lunch (he loved sweets), and I'd tell him to be sure to make some tea or coffee for himself.'*

Thus, he put on weight which, although Sonia was pleased to see, he hated it, referring to himself as a 'porpoise'. She also managed to expand his food interests, taking him out to restaurants, and introducing him to Italian food which became his favorite food. She also took steps to change the way he dressed:

> *I remember so well when I took him to a smart haberdashery how he protested at the newness of the coat and hat I persuaded him to accept and wear. He looked at himself in the mirror and protested, 'But my dear, this is entirely too stylish for 'Grandpa Theobald'; it doesn't look like me. I look like some fashionable fop!' To which I replied, 'Not all men who dress fashionably are necessarily fops.'*

The Kalem Club

The two were still heavily involved with the amateur world. Sonia was president of the UAPA while Lovecraft was editor. And they spent a considerable amount of their free time in the company of other amateurs. Sonia introduced Lovecraft to the Blue Pencil Club in Brooklyn of which he was not overly fond but which he would attend when she was in town. Another was The Writers' Club attended by Lovecraft in March. When

Morton asked him if he would be going in May, Lovecraft responded that 'It all depends on the ball-and-chain.' He added that, 'She generally has to hit the hay early, and I have to get home in proportionate time, since she can't get to sleep till I do.'

Nonetheless, he began to spend increasing amounts of time with his friends. He was part of a group that was informally called the Kalem Club, known as such because all the surnames of the members start with K, L or M. Lovecraft never refers to it as the Kalem Club in his letters, preferring to describe it as 'the boys' or 'the gang'. Members included his friends Kleiner, Morton and Long but others soon joined.

Lovecraft in New York, *c.* 1924.

Arthur Leeds (1882 – 1952?) was an interesting character who had traveled with a circus as a boy and at this point, aged 40, was a columnist for *Writer's Digest* as well as a contributor to pulp magazines. Everett McNeill was also a part of the group as was George Kirk whom Lovecraft had met during his trip to Cleveland. He was a bookseller who in 1922 had published *Twenty-one Letters of Ambrose Bierce,* Samuel Loveman's collection of letters to him from the great writer.

Lovecraft in Full Flow

The Kalem Club was already in existence when Lovecraft arrived in New York but he became the club's fulcrum. Frank Long described a typical get-together but also presents a picture of Lovecraft in full flow:

'Almost invariably ... Howard did most of the talking, at least for the first ten or fifteen minutes. He would sink into an easy chair – he never seemed to feel at ease in a straight-backed chair on such occasions and I took care to keep an extremely comfortable one unoccupied until his arrival – and words would flow from him in a continuous stream. He never seemed to experience the slightest necessity to pause between words. There was no groping about for just the right term, no matter how recondite his conversation became. When the need for some metaphysical hair-splitting arose, it was easy to visualize scissors honed to a surgical sharpness snipping away in the recesses of his mind ... In general the conversation was lively and quite variegated. It was a brilliant enough assemblage, and the discussions ranged from current happenings of a political or sociological nature, to some recent book or play, or to five or six centuries of English and French literature, art, philosophy, and natural science.'

They would meet every Thursday night and afterwards Lovecraft would often spend the depths of the night exploring the architecture of the area. Hart Crane found this especially tiresome and described him as that 'queer Lovecraft fellow'. Lovecraft would return home to Sonia at anything between 5 and 9 a.m. which puts something of a lie to his statement that he had to be home so that she could get to sleep.

Where Night-Black Deeds are Done

Annie Gamwell arrived for a visit on September 21, 1924 and in October, Lovecraft visited the colonial antiquities of Elizabeth, New Jersey. Finally, though, inspired by a building in Elizabeth, he was ready to write again. 'The Shunned House' would be the first story he had written in eight months. He described the source for the building of the title:

'... on the northeast corner of Bridge St. & Elizabeth Ave. is a terrible old house – a hellish place where night-black deeds must have been done in the early seventeen-hundreds – with a blackish unpainted surface, unnaturally steep roof, & an outside flight of steps leading to the second story, suffocatingly embowered in a tangle of ivy so dense that one cannot but imagine it accursed or corpse-fed. It reminded me of the Babbitt House in Benefit St ... Later its image came up again with renewed vividness, finally causing me to write a new horror story with its scene in Providence and with the Babbitt House as its basis.'

Best Thing I Ever Writ

The ending of 'The Shunned House' seems very similar to the ending of Lovecraft's previous story, 'Imprisoned with the Pharaohs', in that what the narrator has seen is merely a small part of a huge creature. But it is a good tale, richly textured and with oodles of historical background to give it a sense of reality. Lovecraft even provides a pseudo-scientific rationale for the existence of the monster. It has been described as one of his best short novels and when he read it to the Kalem Club members, they 'waxed incredibly enthusiastick in affirming that it is the best thing I ever writ.'

'The Shunned House', with the addition of an introduction by Frank Belknap Long, was scheduled to be Lovecraft's first published book. W. Paul Cook printed 250 copies of it in 1928 for Recluse Press, but the sheets were never bound. In 1959, 150 sets of these sheets were obtained by Arkham House. Fifty sets were sold unbound and a hundred were bound. These are now regarded as the 'holy grail' for Lovecraft collectors, selling for many thousands of dollars.

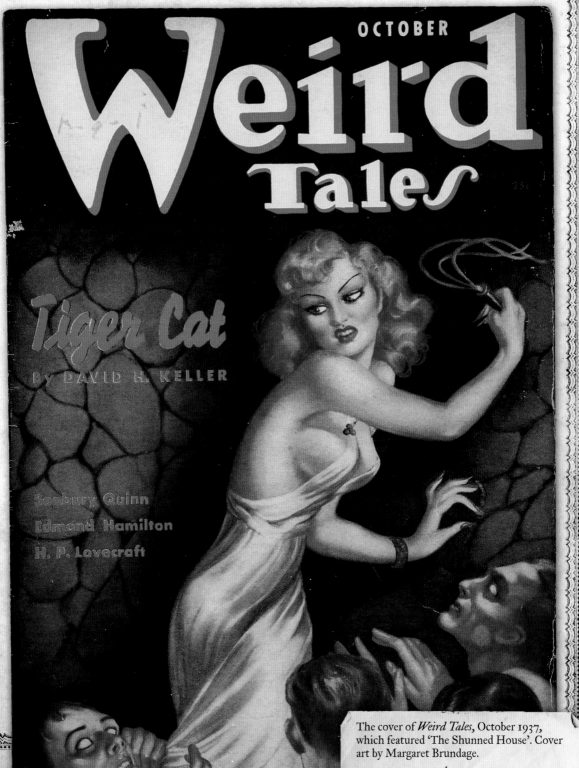

The cover of *Weird Tales*, October 1937, which featured 'The Shunned House'. Cover art by Margaret Brundage.

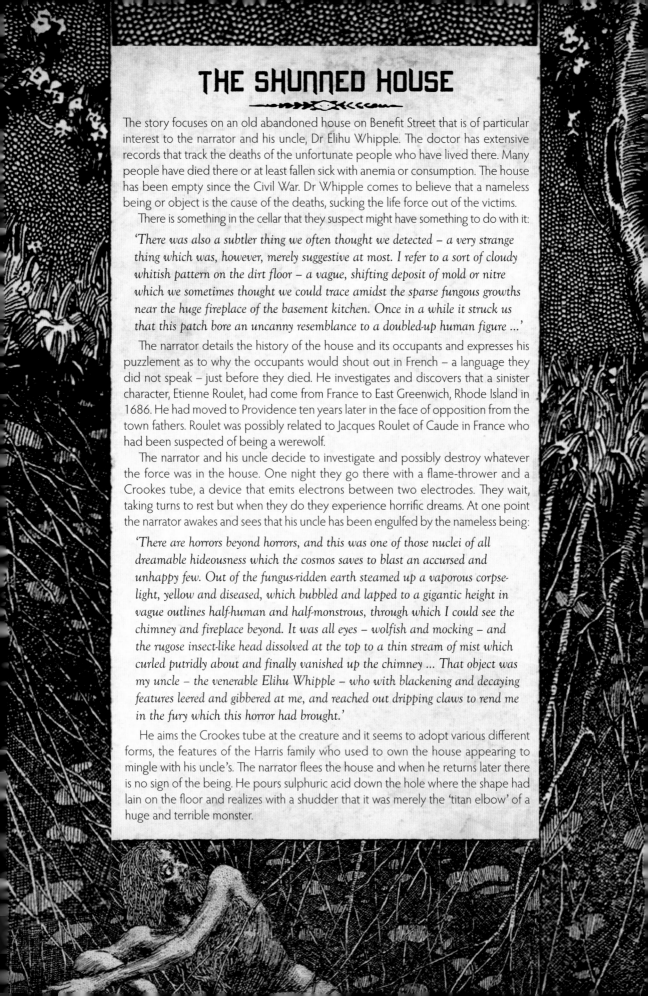

THE SHUNNED HOUSE

The story focuses on an old abandoned house on Benefit Street that is of particular interest to the narrator and his uncle, Dr Elihu Whipple. The doctor has extensive records that track the deaths of the unfortunate people who have lived there. Many people have died there or at least fallen sick with anemia or consumption. The house has been empty since the Civil War. Dr Whipple comes to believe that a nameless being or object is the cause of the deaths, sucking the life force out of the victims.

There is something in the cellar that they suspect might have something to do with it:

'There was also a subtler thing we often thought we detected – a very strange thing which was, however, merely suggestive at most. I refer to a sort of cloudy whitish pattern on the dirt floor – a vague, shifting deposit of mold or nitre which we sometimes thought we could trace amidst the sparse fungous growths near the huge fireplace of the basement kitchen. Once in a while it struck us that this patch bore an uncanny resemblance to a doubled-up human figure ...'

The narrator details the history of the house and its occupants and expresses his puzzlement as to why the occupants would shout out in French – a language they did not speak – just before they died. He investigates and discovers that a sinister character, Etienne Roulet, had come from France to East Greenwich, Rhode Island in 1686. He had moved to Providence ten years later in the face of opposition from the town fathers. Roulet was possibly related to Jacques Roulet of Caude in France who had been suspected of being a werewolf.

The narrator and his uncle decide to investigate and possibly destroy whatever the force was in the house. One night they go there with a flame-thrower and a Crookes tube, a device that emits electrons between two electrodes. They wait, taking turns to rest but when they do they experience horrific dreams. At one point the narrator awakes and sees that his uncle has been engulfed by the nameless being:

'There are horrors beyond horrors, and this was one of those nuclei of all dreamable hideousness which the cosmos saves to blast an accursed and unhappy few. Out of the fungus-ridden earth steamed up a vaporous corpse-light, yellow and diseased, which bubbled and lapped to a gigantic height in vague outlines half-human and half-monstrous, through which I could see the chimney and fireplace beyond. It was all eyes – wolfish and mocking – and the rugose insect-like head dissolved at the top to a thin stream of mist which curled putridly about and finally vanished up the chimney ... That object was my uncle – the venerable Elihu Whipple – who with blackening and decaying features leered and gibbered at me, and reached out dripping claws to rend me in the fury which this horror had brought.'

He aims the Crookes tube at the creature and it seems to adopt various different forms, the features of the Harris family who used to own the house appearing to mingle with his uncle's. The narrator flees the house and when he returns later there is no sign of the being. He pours sulphuric acid down the hole where the shape had lain on the floor and realizes with a shudder that it was merely the 'titan elbow' of a huge and terrible monster.

Main internal illustrations for 'The Shunned House' from *Weird Tales*, October 1937. Artist Virgil Finlay.

Weird Tales, July 1938, interior illustration by Virgil
Finlay (1914 – 1971). American artist Virgil Finlay
was a great science fiction and horror illustrator who,
as well as illustrating Lovecraft's works, created more
than 2,600 pieces of graphic art for pulp magazines in
his 35-year career. His work appeared in 62 issues of
Weird Tales and he also created 19 *Weird Tales* covers.
Finlay was inducted into the Science Fiction Hall of
Fame in 2012.

CHAPTER 8

LIVING APART

Clinton Street

On December 31, 1924, Sonia took the train to Cincinnati to take up her department-store position. They had lived together for only ten months and she would only return to New York at intervals over the next fifteen months, spending a total of thirteen weeks of that time with her husband. Her absence did not make much difference to Lovecraft. In fact, according to his journal, he positively enjoyed his temporary bachelor status, having the freedom and the peace to write whenever he wanted.

The day that Sonia left, Lovecraft had moved into a large room on the first floor of a house in Clinton Street in the Brooklyn Heights area of New York City. He had probably found it with the help of his Aunt Lillian who came to visit in December. A description of the room can be read in the diary that he kept in 1925:

'On December 31, 1924, I established myself in a large room of pleasing & tasteful proportions at 169 Clinton St., cor. of State, in the Heights or Borough Hall section of Brooklyn, in an house of early Victorian date with white classic woodwork & tall windows with panel'd seats. Two alcoves with portieres enable one to preserve the pure library effect & the whole forms a pleasing hermitage for an old-fashion'd man, with its generous view of ancient brick houses in State & Clinton Sts.'

He furnished the room with seven bookcases that lined the room's two walls, a desk, a few chairs, a table in the center of the room and a sofa-bed. There was nowhere to cook a meal. This suited Lovecraft who could not cook anyway and was pleased not to have to wash up. He had no trouble keeping the place clean: 'I dust only once in three days, sweep only once a week, & eat so simply that I

seldom have to do any dishwashing beyond a simple plate, or cup & saucer, plus one or two metallic utensils.' The room had two alcoves, one for washing and one for dressing. The location was not great but was at least served by subway trains that he was pleased to note ran all night – highly useful to him when he was returning from one of his nocturnal perambulations.

Still, he was paying only $40 a month for it and he spent little more than $5 a week on food, surviving on bread and eating cold food out of cans. Eventually, he had to purchase an oil heater that not only warmed his room but also served as a makeshift cooker for his tins. However, he lost a great deal of weight as a result of his diet, dropping from almost 200 pounds to 146. His collar size dropped from size 16 to size 14½.

Seeking Gainful Employment

Things were not going well for Sonia. Her job at Mabley & Carew's had the benefit of allowing her to make monthly trips to New York but by late February she was no longer employed by them. Lovecraft wrote to his aunts that she had found 'the hostile & exacting atmosphere of Mabley & Carew's intolerable; finally being virtually forced out of her position by quibbling executives & invidious inferiors.'

She was in New York for an extended period in February and March but she was still not entirely well and decided to take the six weeks' rest advocated earlier by her doctors, spending from late March to early June in Saratoga Springs in upstate New York. She returned to Brooklyn for June and July but, finding work in a hat shop in Cleveland, she left on July 24, 1925. That job, too, had gone by mid-October when she took up a position with Halle's, Cleveland's top department store. She remained there until late 1926.

Lovecraft's job-seeking, on the other hand was fairly desultory and was dependent, largely, on tips from friends. He did some work writing advertising copy but was not terribly good at it. The company folded, however, around the end of July. He also thought he might have landed a position as James Morton's assistant at the Paterson Museum but nothing ever came of it. What money he did earn came from the sale of stories to *Weird Tales*, five being published in 1925. He received $35 for 'The Festival' in January's issue; $25 for 'The Unnamable' in July; and $50 for 'The Temple' in September. We do not know how much he was paid for the other two – 'The Statement of Randolph Carter' in February and 'The Music of Erich Zann' in May.

Living Beyond His Means

This was obviously insufficient to cover his expenses and it must be surmised that Sonia was providing financial support as well as Lillian and Annie who were themselves not well off, living, as they did, off their inheritance from Whipple Phillips. Nonetheless, they were sending him $15 a week. Sonia, meanwhile was paying for food, fares, laundry and his writing materials and whenever she visited she left a decent sum of money with him. It cost Lovecraft around $990 a year to live and he was himself only bringing in around $250 of that from his stories and from mortgage payments of around $74 that he received as part of his inheritance.

The absence of work, of course, gave him more time for visiting friends, which he did on a virtually daily basis. He even had a key to Samuel Loveman's apartment. They met in each other's rooms or at various cafeterias and automats in Manhattan or Brooklyn. But, of course, there were also the Wednesday meetings. He was so busy, in fact, with all of this, plus UAPA business, that he wrote no

more than a handful of poems during the first seven months of 1925. He did not even write very many letters to his aunts. Finally, in August 1925, he penned three short stories one after the other: 'The Horror at Red Hook', 'He' and 'In the Vault'.

A Hopeless Tangle and Enigma

'The Horror at Red Hook', a tale of devil worship and human sacrifice, was written on the first two days of August. Red Hook is a small peninsula about two miles southwest of where Lovecraft lived and the story arose out of his nocturnal wanderings with 'the boys'. He describes the area in the story as 'a maze of hybrid squalour', as having 'the alluring antique flavor which conventional reading

Lovecraft holding Frank Belknap Long's cat, Felis, Brooklyn, *c.* 1925.

THE HORROR AT RED HOOK

'The Horror at Red Hook' features a Dublin-born detective, Thomas F. Malone from the Borough Hall police station who, at the beginning of the story, undergoes a brief nervous attack that makes him issue 'a series of terrified, hysterical shrieks' and run frantically down the street. The cause of his fit was a case he had worked on in which buildings had collapsed, killing a number of police officers. He is now under medical supervision and ordered to avoid tall buildings. However, there is more to his malaise than just collapsing buildings.

'What could he tell the prosaic of the antique witcheries and grotesque marvels discernible to sensitive eyes amidst the poison cauldron where all the varied dregs of unwholesome ages mix their venom and perpetuate their obscene terrors? He had seen the hellish green flame of secret wonder in this blatant, evasive welter of outward greed and inward blasphemy, and had smiled gently when all the New-Yorkers he knew scoffed at his experiment in police work. They had been very witty and cynical, deriding his fantastic pursuit of unknowable mysteries and assuring him that in these days New York held nothing but cheapness and vulgarity.'

The case Malone had been investigating was that of Robert Suydam, a Red Hook recluse who suddenly seemed to look younger and had become engaged to a well-off woman. Meanwhile, the area was suffering a spate of kidnappings. Suydam had been importing strange books from Europe and had been visited every night by 'odd delegations of mixed rowdies and foreigners'. There appeared to be some type of ritual being carried out in his flat. Summoned to court, however, no wrongdoing could be proved against him.

Suydam married the woman but as he and his bride were leaving New York on a ship, a scream was heard. Entering Suydam's stateroom, a sailor found him and his wife dead and there was a claw-mark on the throat of Mrs. Suydam who had been strangled. Police officers visited Suydam's flat and found a cellar door that Malone broke open. Immediately, he was sucked inside:

'A crack formed and enlarged, and the whole door gave way – but from the other side; whence poured a howling tumult of ice-cold wind with all the stenches of the bottomless pit, and whence reached a sucking force not of earth or heaven, which, coiling sentiently about the paralyzed detective, dragged him through the aperture and down unmeasured spaces filled with whispers and wails, and gusts of mocking laughter.'

Suydam's body had been handed over to a group of suspicious characters whose leader was 'an Arab with a hatefully negroid mouth', (Lovecraft not missing any opportunity to racially slur). Eventually, Malone had been found in the basement, the building having collapsed above him, trapping and killing everyone inside.

First published in *Weird Tales*, January 1927, 'The Horror at Red Hook' also appeared in *Weird Tales*, March 1952 issue which included Jon Arfstrom's great illustration above.

leads us to call "Dickensian".' The real heart of the story's intention comes in a further description:

> *The population is a hopeless tangle and enigma; Syrian, Spanish, Italian, and negro elements impinging on one another, and fragments of Scandinavian and American belts lying not far distant. It is a babel of sound and filth, and sends out strange cries to answer the lapping of oily waves at its grimy piers and the monstrous organ litanies of the harbor whistles.'*

The story is a racist rant aimed squarely at the 'foreigners' that have 'stolen' New York from people of white Anglo-Saxon stock.

Sonia later described how angry he would become when the couple found themselves in a mixed race crowd:

> *'... he became livid with rage at the foreign elements he would see in large number, especially at noon-time, in the streets of New York City, and I would try to calm his outbursts by saying: "You don't have to love them; but hating them so outrageously can't do any good." It was then that he said: "It is more important to know what to hate than it is to know what to love." '*

In 'The Horror at Red Hook' he writes of 'Brooklyn's gangs of young loafers and herds of evil looking foreigners' and uses phrases

LOVECRAFT'S RACISM

One disagreeable trait that Lovecraft possessed throughout his life – one shared with his father and other members of his family – was that of racism. He displayed contempt and even disgust for black people and Jews but his racism also took in Asians, Arabs, Mexicans, Italians, the Irish and Poles. It is little defense to point out that there were numerous pseudo-scientific theories at the time that promoted the notion that black people were inherently inferior to whites.

Corresponding with his friend Rheinhart Kleiner on November 16, 1916, he wrote:

> *'Hope Street is near enough to them North End [an area of Providence that was home to a sizable Jewish community] to have a considerable Jewish attendance. It was there that I formed my intractable aversion to the Semitic race. The Jews were brilliant in their classes – calculatingly and schemingly brilliant – but their ideals were sordid and their manners coarse. I became rather well known as an anti-Semite before I had been at Hope Street many days.'*

The irony was that he married a Jew in Sonia Greene and one of his closest friends, Samuel Loveman, was also Jewish. Sonia was often subject to his racist tirades and often had to remind him that it was not acceptable to speak in such a way in public. Sadly, his views did not mellow with age and living in the melting pot of New York in the 1920s, a teeming metropolis filled with immigrants of many hues and

races, often drove him to distraction. In a letter of the 1920s, he disgracefully described how 'loathsome Asiatic hordes trail their dirty carcasses over streets where white men once moved, and air their odious presence and twisted visage and stunted forms till we shall be driven either to murder them or emigrate ourselves … It is not good for a proud, light-skinned Nordic to be cast away alone amongst squat, squint-eyed jabberers with coarse ways and alien emotions whom his deepest cell tissue hates and loathes as the mammal hates and loathes the reptile, with an instinct as old as history.'

Indeed racist sentiments can be found in his stories 'The Horror at Red Hook' – described by the English fantasy fiction writer, China Miéville, as 'extraordinarily racist' – and the following passage from 'Herbert West – Reanimator':

> *'He was a loathsome, gorilla-like thing, with abnormally long arms that I could not help calling fore legs, and a face that conjured up thoughts of unspeakable Congo secrets and tom-tom poundings under an eerie moon. The body must have looked even worse in life – but the world holds many ugly things.'*

Miéville adds, '[Lovecraft's racism] goes further, in my opinion, than "merely" *being* a racist – I follow Michel Houellebecq … in thinking that Lovecraft's oeuvre, his work itself, is inspired by and deeply structured with race hatred. As Houellebecq said, it is racism itself that raises in Lovecraft a "poetic trance".'

such as 'Asian dregs', 'primitive half-ape savagery' and 'unclassified slant-eyed folk'. It has to be said, however, that in the world of pulp fiction at that time, he was not alone in including such racist sentiments in his stories.

Lovecraft's absence from the typewriter for all those months shows in the poor quality of his writing in 'The Horror at Red Hook'. He certainly did not think it was very good. Lin Carter describes it as 'a piece of literary vitriol' and others have been put off by the story's racism. The Lovecraft expert, S.T. Joshi called it 'horrendously bad'.

Labyrinths of Ancient Streets

His next story, 'He', is a tale of sadness and loss, written as Lovecraft sat in Scott Park,

New Jersey. He had been up wandering all the previous night and around seven in the morning boarded a ferry to Elizabeth, New Jersey. There, he bought a notebook, went to Scott Park and wrote the story.

It appears that the genesis of the story lay in a meeting he and Sonia had with an old man who offered to take them on a tour of Greenwich Village. At one point, he led them into a hidden courtyard that dated back to the Colonial period.

There is much to admire in 'He' – its brooding atmosphere and the apocalyptic visions of the future that so horrify the narrator, for example. This story and another, 'The Cats of Ulthar' were accepted by Farnsworth Wright for *Weird Tales* and 'He' appeared in the magazine's September 1926 edition.

HE

The story opens with what one can only presume was a piece of heart-wrenching autobiographical writing from Lovecraft:

> 'My coming to New York had been a mistake; for whereas I had looked for poignant wonder and inspiration in the teeming labyrinths of ancient streets that twist endlessly from forgotten courts and squares and waterfronts to courts and squares and waterfronts equally forgotten, and in the Cyclopean modern towers and pinnacles that rise blackly Babylonian and under waning moons, I had found instead only a sense of horror and oppression which threatened to master, paralyze, and annihilate me.'

The narrator has moved, like Lovecraft, from New England to New York. One night while walking through an old part of Greenwich Village, he encounters a stranger who seems to be dressed in the manner of a man from the eighteenth century. As had happened with Lovecraft and Sonia, the man offers to show the narrator the secrets of the area. The stranger takes the narrator to his home where he tells him the story of a man who a hundred years earlier had tricked some native Americans into divulging the secrets of time and space. He had then poisoned them with bad whisky.

By the end of the week, he was the only person

left alive who possessed these secrets. The stranger then confesses that he is, in fact, that man. The narrator, naturally, does not believe him but when the stranger shows him horrific visions of the future to prove the truth of what he has said, the narrator begins to scream. These screams awaken the spirits of the Native Americans the stranger had killed and they take revenge on him:

> 'In those greenish beams the candles paled, and a new semblance of decay spread over the musk-reeking room with its wormy paneling, sagging floor, battered mantel, rickety furniture, and ragged draperies. It spread over the old man, too, whether from the same source or because of his fear and vehemence, and I saw him shrivel and blacken as he lurched near and strove to rend me with vulturine talons. Only his eyes stayed whole, and they glared with a propulsive, dilated incandescence which grew as the face around them charred and dwindled.'

Escaping, the narrator flees New York and returns home:

> '... the city is dead and full of unsuspected horrors. Whither he has gone, I do not know; but I have gone home to the pure New England lanes up which fragrant sea-winds sweep at evening.'

The Birth of Cthulhu

After a meeting of the Kalem Club on Wednesday, August 12, 1925, Lovecraft went home to Clinton Street and immediately began sketching out a new novelette, 'The Call of Cthulhu'. It would take him a year to get down to the writing of this story that would become one of the most important pieces of fiction he would pen. He pointed out to Lillian in a letter that such a lengthy piece of writing 'ought to bring in a very decent-sized cheque'.

Meanwhile, he received a plot idea from C.W. Smith, the editor of *Tryout* amateur magazine. Lovecraft described it as being about 'an undertaker imprisoned in a village vault where he was removing winter coffins for spring burial, & his escape by enlarging a transom reached by the piling up of the coffins'.

Lovecraft standing in front of 169 Clinton Street, Brooklyn, 1925.

On September 18, he turned this plot outline into his third story in two months – 'In the Vault'. It was rejected by *Weird Tales* in November 1925, Lovecraft saying that Farnsworth Wright was afraid 'its extreme gruesomeness would not pass the Indiana censorship', an obvious reference to the scandal created by 'The Loved Dead'. It was also rejected in August 1926 by the pulp magazine *Ghost Stories*. Eventually, *Weird Tales* published it in April 1932.

Going Home

Lovecraft may around this time have been coming to a decision to leave New York and return to Providence, but he had not said as much to Sonia. He even suggested to one of his circle that the temporary separation from his wife might become a permanent one, although there was no mention of divorce. Eventually, he announced to his friends that he planned to return to Providence the following spring.

Meanwhile, in Cleveland, Sonia was once more out of work by October 1925, but found another position almost immediately. Unfortunately, her work schedule made it impossible for her to travel back to New York before the middle of January 1926.

Terror and Weirdness

In the middle of November, Lovecraft received an interesting commission from the writer and publisher, W. Paul Cook who had launched a new magazine, the *Recluse*. It was 'an article on the element of terror & weirdness in literature', as Lovecraft put it. The article would take eighteen months to write and would emerge as 'Supernatural Horror in Literature', a critical survey of supernatural fiction.

Lovecraft threw himself into it, re-reading all the major – and minor – works, re-familiarizing himself with many of his favorite authors, as well as many for whom he did not have such a soft spot. For example, he

COOL AIR

The narrator has obtained some magazine work in New York and has moved into a run-down boarding house with a Spanish landlady. In the apartment above lives Dr Muñoz, a reclusive retired medical man who has a laboratory filled with chemicals and always maintains a temperature of 55 degrees in his rooms.

One day, the narrator suffers a heart attack as he is working in his room and drags himself upstairs to seek medical help from the doctor. Muñoz administers drugs to him and saves his life, beginning a friendship with the narrator.

The narrator visits Muñoz often in his room and learns of the doctor's obsession with defeating death. '… he was the bitterest of sworn enemies to death, and had sunk his fortune and lost all his friends in a lifetime of bizarre experiment devoted to its bafflement and extirpation.' As time passes, the doctor's health declines and he becomes increasingly odd. The temperature in the rooms is reduced to sub-freezing so that the narrator has to wear a thick coat when he visits. One night the pump on the machine that produces the cool air malfunctions and, panic-stricken, the doctor pleads with the narrator to help him.

Unfortunately, it cannot be repaired until morning, forcing the doctor to remain in a bathtub filled with ice procured by the narrator. He recruits someone else to fetch the ice while he goes in search of a new pump, but on his return finds the house in uproar.

Black terror, however, had preceded me. The house was in utter turmoil, and above the chatter of awed voices I heard a man praying in a deep basso. Fiendish things were in the air, and

lodgers told over the beads of their rosaries as they caught the odor from beneath the doctor's closed door. The lounger I had hired, it seems, had fled screaming and mad-eyed not long after his second delivery of ice; perhaps as a result of excessive curiosity. He could not, of course, have locked the door behind him; yet it was now fastened, presumably from the inside. There was no sound within save a nameless sort of slow, thick dripping.

Entering the apartment, the narrator finds the horrifically decomposed remains of the doctor. A letter has been left from which the narrator learns Muñoz's secret. He had actually died eighteen years previously but had used various techniques to keep his body going, one of which was cool air.

'The end,' ran that noisome scrawl, 'is here. No more ice – the man looked and ran away. Warmer every minute, and the tissues can't last. I fancy you know – what I said about the will and the nerves and the preserved body after the organs ceased to work. It was good theory, but couldn't keep up indefinitely. There was a gradual deterioration I had not foreseen. Dr. Torres knew, but the shock killed him. He couldn't stand what he had to do – he had to get me in a strange, dark place when he minded my letter and nursed me back. And the organs never would work again. It had to be done my way– artificial preservation – for you see I died that time eighteen years ago.'

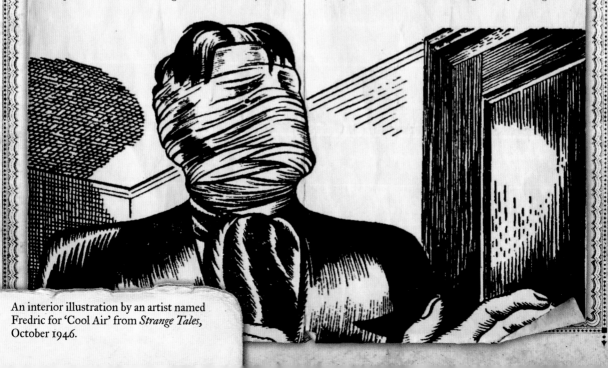

An interior illustration by an artist named Fredric for 'Cool Air' from *Strange Tales*, October 1946.

spent three days reading the works of E.T.A. Hoffmann in the New York Public Library, even though he found him exceedingly dull and he was given a mere half-paragraph in the final work. The piece would cover from the earliest examples of this kind of writing, from Graeco-Roman times right up to the modern masters – Dunsany, Poe, Blackwood, Machen, Bierce and M.R. James.

Writing 'Supernatural Horror in Literature' was undoubtedly very good for Lovecraft. 'It's a good preparation for composing a new series of weird tales of my own,' he wrote. It also gave him something to focus on and brought an end to the aimless wandering of the previous few years. The first fruit of this new resolve was a story named 'Cool Air', possibly the best story of his New York period.

'Cool Air' contains brilliantly understated writing. Lovecraft, it seemed was holding back and it is very effective in creating suspense and an atmosphere of increasing dread. Farnsworth Wright disagreed, however, rejecting 'Cool Air', because it was 'too grisly' which is odd, because it seems to be just the kind of tale he normally went for. It is a story that has since been adapted many times, on three occasions for film and television.

No Prospect of Rescue

Sonia spent between February 15 and March 5, 1925 in New York and would not be able to return until June if things continued to go well in her job. Loveman found some work for Lovecraft, addressing envelopes at a bookshop and earning $17.50 a week for three weeks.

Lovecraft described himself, of course, in 'Cool Air', but he was tiring of Clinton Street and New York. In letters to his aunts, he speaks of his despair, how he had been 'screaming in sheer desperation and pounding the walls and floor'. Eventually, Frank Belknap Long became so concerned about his friend's state of mind that he asked his mother to write to Lillian and tell her about the state her nephew was in. Mrs Long wrote that she feared he 'might go off the deep end'. Long later wrote:

'My mother quickly realized that his sanity might indeed be imperiled if another month passed without a prospect of rescue and wrote a long letter to his aunts, describing the situation in detail. I doubt whether Sonia even knew about that letter. At least she never mentioned it in recalling that particular period.'

Lillian responded immediately, sending a cheque to Lovecraft to buy a train ticket back to Providence.

LOVECRAFT'S DEFINITION OF A WEIRD TALE

The true weird tale has something more than secret murder, bloody bones, or a sheeted form clanking chains according to rule. A certain atmosphere of breathless and unexplainable dread of outer, unknown forces must be present; and there must be a hint, expressed with a seriousness and portentousness becoming of its subject, of that most terrible conception of the human brain – a malign and particular suspension or defeat of those fixed laws of Nature which are our only safeguard against the assaults of chaos and the daemons of unplumbed space … Atmosphere is the all-important thing, for the final criterion of authenticity is not the dovetailing of a plot but the creation of a given sensation … Therefore, we must judge a weird tale … by the emotional level which it attains at its least mundane point … The one test of the really weird is simply this – whether or not there be excited in the reader a profound sense of dread, and of contact with unknown spheres and powers … And, of course, the more completely and unifiedly a story conveys this atmosphere the better it is as a work of art in the given medium.

CHAPTER 9

RETURN TO PROVIDENCE

Home Again

Lovecraft wrote to Lillian around April 1925, probably in response to an invitation by her to pay her and Annie a visit.

> '... I couldn't bear to see Providence again till I can be there for ever. When I do get home, I shall hesitate about going even to Pawtucket or East Providence, whilst the thought of crossing into Massachusetts at Hunt's Mills fills me with positive horror! But a temporary glimpse would be like that of a distrest mariner swept by a storm within sight of his own harbor, then washed away again into the illimitable blackness of an alien sea.'

In November 1925, he wrote, 'My mental life is really at home,' by which he meant Providence. He had never really left. Throughout his time in New York, Lillian paid for a subscription for him to the *Providence Evening Bulletin*. He also maintained his studies of Providence history.

As his New York sojourn drew to a close, Lovecraft's enthusiastic socializing became a thing of the past. Sometimes when one of 'the boys' would come knocking at his door in Clinton Street, he failed to answer it, pretending to be out. He justified such behavior in a letter to Lillian – 'I am essentially a recluse who will have very little to do with people wherever he may be.' He had never entirely lost his feeling of being an outsider in society – '... most people only make me nervous ... it makes no difference how well they mean or how cordial they are, they simply get on my nerves.'

Finally on April 17, 1926 he returned to Providence, the move evidently having been sanctioned by Sonia. 'S H endorses the move most thoroughly,' he wrote, 'had a marvelously magnanimous letter from her yesterday.' Lillian had found a place

for herself and Lovecraft for $10 a week, at 10 Barnes Street, a three-storey Victorian house close to the Brown University campus. At Barnes Street, he occupied the ground floor while Lillian took a room on the second floor.

Ecstasy and Euphoria

Sonia appeared to be happy to help him move from Brooklyn but did not seem terribly keen to move to Providence herself. She wrote later, 'He wanted more than anything else to go back to Providence but he also wanted *me* to come along, and this I could not do because there was no situation open there for me; that is, one fitting my ability and my need.' Sonia arrived in New York on Sunday, April 11, 1926 and the packing was done by April 13. One last meeting of the Kalem Club followed and after a final nocturnal tour with Kirk, Lovecraft left New York.

He was euphoric to be home and expressed his joy in a description of the arrival in Providence in a letter to Long, the writing getting bigger the closer he got to Providence:

> '... Auburn – just outside the city limits – I fumble with bags & wraps in a desperate effort to keep calm – THEN – a delirious marble dome outside the window – a hissing of air brakes – a slackening of speed – surges of ecstasy & dropping of clouds from my eyes & mind – HOME – UNION STATION – PROVIDENCE!!!!'

The last eleven years of Lovecraft's life could now begin and during them he proved the truth of a famous remark by W. Paul Cook: 'He came back to Providence a human being – and what a human being! He had been tried in the fire and came out pure gold.'

The Black Seas of Infinity

We know little of what Lovecraft did during those first few months at home. Information becomes more difficult now as, of course, he was no longer writing regular letters to his aunts. But soon he would spring into life and enjoy an astonishing production of fiction, some of the best of his career. Between the summer of 1926 and the spring of 1927 he produced two short novels, two novelettes and three short stories.

In the summer of 1926 he dug out the sketch of 'The Call of Cthulhu', the outline of which he had drafted the previous year. There are undoubtedly connections in this tale with Lovecraft's experiences in New York, his feeling of being an alien in a hostile world. He really had feared that he would lose his mind if he had remained there. After all, he would not be the first member of his family to do so.

Creating a Modern Myth

Once again, Farnsworth Wright initially rejected the story, but when Lovecraft's friend, Donald Wandrei told him that Lovecraft was thinking of submitting it to another magazine, he hurriedly accepted it for *Weird Tales*. It was published in February 1928 and is regarded as one of Lovecraft's greatest works.

Conan-creator Robert E. Howard described 'The Call of Cthulhu' as 'a masterpiece, which I am sure will live as one of the highest achievements in literature.' Celebrated French writer, Michel Houellebecq, cites it in his book, *H.P. Lovecraft: Against the World, Against Life* as the first of Lovecraft's 'great texts'. Lovecraft himself considered the story to be 'rather middling – not as bad as the worst, but full of cheap and cumbrous touches.'

THE CALL OF CTHULHU
(FOUND AMONG THE PAPERS OF THE LATE FRANCIS WAYLAND THURSTON, OF BOSTON)

The story begins with the immortal lines:

'The most merciful thing in the world ... is the inability of the human mind to correlate all its contents. We live on a placid island of ignorance in the midst of black seas of infinity, and it was not meant that we should voyage far.'

The text is from notes that have been found, written by Francis Wayland Thurston from the papers of his uncle, George Gammell Angell as well as from his own investigations. Angell, a professor of Semitic languages at Brown University, had taken notes on the dreams of a young sculptor, Henry Anthony Wilcox. Wilcox had brought to him a bas-relief of an ugly alien being that he had sculpted in his sleep on March 1, 1925. In the dream he had that night he had heard the repeated words 'Cthulhu fhtagn'.

Angell became very interested because he had heard these words years previously at a meeting of the American Archaeological Society. A New Orleans police inspector, John Raymond Legrasse had brought to that meeting a similar sculpture and said that it had been worshipped by a degenerate cult in the Louisiana bayou. They had chanted the sounds '*Ph'nglui mglw'nafh Cthulhu R'lyeh wgah'nagl fhtagn.*' This meant 'In his house at R'lyeh dead Cthulhu waits dreaming.'

Legrasse was told that Cthulhu was, in fact, a huge being that had traveled to the earth from the stars millennia ago, accompanied by another set of creatures known as the Great Old Ones. He was buried in the sunken city of R'lyeh and would awake when the 'stars were ready'. This information, apparently, can all be read in the *Necronomicon* written by the mad Arab Abdul Alhazred.

Thurston finds a newspaper clipping that talks about strange events that occurred on a ship in the Pacific Ocean. The newspaper cutting features a picture of a similar statue to the one sculpted by Wilcox and found in Louisiana. He travels to Oslo to speak to the only survivor of that ship's crew, a man named Gustav Johansen, but finds when he arrives that Johansen is dead.

However, he has left behind an account of what happened on the ship and details encountering Cthulhu when R'lyeh rose from the depths during an earthquake. However, the city had sunk again, circumstances not being right for the return of Cthulhu. Having finished reading the manuscript, Thurston realizes that he must now be a target.

'As my uncle went, as poor Johansen went, so I shall go. I know too much, and the cult still lives.'

Lovecraft's opinion notwithstanding, there is a new assurance and confidence in 'Cthulhu'. His writing has matured and this maturity would color the work of this last, glorious period of his career. He created in 'Cthulhu' a modern myth that has stood the test of time and spawned countless imitations as well as films, videos and board and computer games.

It also constituted a major contribution to what would come to be known as the Cthulhu Mythos. There are many of the elements that would be re-visited by Lovecraft and that would be used by other contributors to the Mythos. There are cross-references in many of his later tales that help to build up an increasing body of myth. But, of course, Lovecraft knew nothing of the Cthulhu Mythos. The term was coined after his death by August Derleth who became his unofficial literary executor.

The Price of a Changeling

In September 1926, Lovecraft wrote another story, 'Pickman's Model'. Compared with the cosmicism of 'Cthulhu', it is no more than a standard story of the supernatural. It uses an unfamiliar technique for Lovecraft – the first person narrative is delivered in the form of a monologue and the person delivering the monologue responds as if someone is asking him questions.

Compared to some of Lovecraft's recent work, 'Pickman's Model' was pretty mundane. It shows the influence of Poe but the ending is, as one critic put it, rather contrived. However, it was just the right kind of tale for Farnsworth Wright at *Weird Tales* who accepted it immediately and published it in the October 1927 issue.

The Cancer of Superstition

In the middle of September 1926, Lovecraft was somewhat surprisingly back in New York. The main purpose of the visit was to see Sonia. She had given up her job in Cleveland and returned to the city so that she could spend weekends with Lovecraft in Providence, but this never happened. She found a job in Chicago in July and was back in New York every couple of weeks on business. They took a room at the Astor Hotel in Manhattan. Needless to say, she worked a great deal of the time she was there and Lovecraft hung out with 'the boys'.

Lovecraft was at this time up to his eyes in revision work for various clients and, of course, corresponding with his many friends. One piece of work was the revision of *The Cancer of Superstition*, a book attacking astrology, for Harry Houdini on which he collaborated with C.M. Eddy. It was something of a rush job but paid $75. Nothing survives of it, apart from an outline by Lovecraft and Eddy's opening pages. Unfortunately, Houdini died suddenly later that same month and the project ended.

The Lands of Lost Dreams

His next piece of fiction was 'The Silver Key', written in early November and informed by a trip he and his Aunt Annie made to his ancestral area of Foster, a place he had not visited since 1908. He loved meeting family members who spoke of Whipple Phillips.

The protagonist, Randolph Carter, also features in 'The Statement of Randolph Carter' and 'The Unnamable'. He will also appear in *The Dream-Quest of Unknown Kadath*, and a sequel to 'The Silver Key' co-written by Lovecraft and E. Hoffmann Price between October 1932 and April 1933.

The story could be said to be 'Dunsanian' in style due to its dream-like element, but there is little else about it that confirms this. In effect, in this story, Lovecraft is fictionalizing his own personal philosophy, attacking literary realism and conventional religion in Carter's attempts to forge a new life for himself. Eventually, it is a return to childhood that saves him. But, of course, the story is redolent of his trip to his ancestral home and his love of New England.

PICKMAN'S MODEL

Boston artist, Richard Upton Pickman, is a painter of horrific images that are magnificently executed but are too graphic by far for the Boston Art Club which revokes his membership. The narrator has not long ago cut himself off from Pickman but the artist has, anyway, recently disappeared.

The story tells how before his disappearance Pickman had taken the narrator on a tour of his personal gallery. The rooms had grown increasingly evil, the paintings more and more horrific. The last room had contained a hideous painting of a red-eyed, canine-looking humanoid chewing on a human victim:

'Listen – can you fancy a squatting circle of nameless dog-like things in a churchyard teaching a small child how to feed like themselves? The price of a changeling, I suppose – you know the old myth about how the weird people leave their spawn in cradles in exchange for the human babes they steal. Pickman was shewing what happens to those stolen babes – how they grow up – and then I began to see a hideous relationship in the faces of the human and non-human figures. He was, in all his gradations of morbidity between the frankly non-human and the degradedly human, establishing a sardonic linkage and evolution. The dog-things were developed from mortals!'

There was a noise and Pickman headed out of the room with a gun. Meanwhile, the narrator had unfolded a piece of paper that he found attached to the hideous painting. There was the sound of shots after which Pickman had re-entered, claiming to have shot some rats. The two men left, but the narrator had realized later that he had stuffed the piece of paper in his pocket when Pickman returned.

'Well – that paper wasn't a photograph of any background, after all. What it shewed was simply the monstrous being he was painting on that awful canvas. It was the model he was using – and its background was merely the wall of the cellar studio in minute detail. But by God, Eliot, it was a photograph from life.'

'Pickman's Model' illustrated by Hannes Bok from *Famous Fantastic Mysteries*, December 1951.

AQUELARRE (WITCHES' SABBATH)
BY FRANCISCO GOYA (1746 – 1828)

Witches' Sabbath is one of Goya's Black Paintings produced between 1819 and 1823, featuring scenes of violence, witches and monsters. In 'Pickman's Model' Lovecraft refers to many artists whom he admired including Goya. Since most of Goya's work was still in Spain, where Lovecraft had never traveled, he may have known him only by reputation.

THE SILVER KEY

Now aged 50, Randolph Carter has lost the key to the gate of dreams that had gained him entry in 'nightly excursions to strange and ancient cities beyond space, and lovely, unbelievable garden lands across ethereal seas.' As he has got older, he has lost the means of enjoying his fantastic journeys:

> 'No more could his galleys sail up the river Oukranos past the gilded spires of Thran, or his elephant caravans tramp through perfumed jungles in Kled, where forgotten palaces with veined ivory columns sleep lovely and unbroken under the moon.'

He has tried to focus instead on reality and tries religion without success. He has even fought throughout the First World War for the Foreign Legion, but it 'stirred him but little.' Writing fails him as does dabbling in the occult. He begins to search out ever more bizarre books and people.

He returns to 'Arkham, the terrible witch-haunted old town of his forefathers in New England, and had experiences in the dark, amidst the hoary willows and tottering gambrel roofs, which made him seal forever certain pages in the diary of a wild-minded ancestor.'

Now he has realized the 'futility of real things' and lives with his 'memories of a dream-filled youth' in contemplative retirement. One night his grandfather reminds him of a great key that had been handed down from his ancestors and now lay in a carved oak box that has lain unopened for two centuries. A servant forces the box open and Carter finds the key and a discolored parchment.

He had previously seen characters like the ones on the parchment on a papyrus scroll owned by an old man he had met in the south. The old man had vanished one night in a cemetery. Feeling himself pulled towards 'some hidden and ancestral source', he travels north 'where haunted Arkham and the rushing Miskatonic and the lonely rustic homestead of his people lay'. He encounters an old family servant, Benijah, but Carter has somehow been transformed into his 9 year-old self. The old servant warns him:

> 'Ye'd orta know these here woods ain't no fitten place to be traipsin' this hour! They's things abroad what dun't do nobody no good, as my gran'sir' knowed afur me. Come, Mister Randy, or Hannah wun't keep supper no longer!'

The servant leads him to the house where his Aunt Martha stands in the doorway. Having eaten and slept, he ventures out, finding a cave, known by locals as the 'snake pen'. He crawls in and pulls the silver key from his pocket.

A search is launched for Carter and his car is found en route to the ruins of the Carter homestead and in it is an old box and a strange parchment. At the homestead it is evident that someone has been there and Carter's handkerchief is found. The narrator does not believe Carter is dead, believing the key has permitted him to return to the 'lands of dream he had lost'. He says that he expects to meet him soon as a new king:

> 'on the opal throne in Ilek-Vad, that fabulous town of turrets atop the hollow cliffs of glass overlooking the twilight sea wherein the bearded and finny Gnorri build their singular labyrinths, and I believe I know how to interpret this rumour. Certainly, I look forward impatiently to the sight of that great silver key, for in its cryptical arabesques there may stand symbolized all the aims and mysteries of a blindly impersonal cosmos.'

The Silver Key that could open the gate to the land of lost dreams.

Needless to say, Farnsworth Wright rejected it, but in the summer of 1928, having asked to have another look at it, he accepted it, paying Lovecraft $70. It appeared in the January 1929 edition of *Weird Tales*, but Wright reported to Lovecraft that readers 'violently disliked' it.

A Far-Forgotten First Youth

In the fall of 1926, Lovecraft started *The Dream-Quest of Unknown Kadath*, finishing it in January 1927. It was never published during his lifetime as he was never entirely satisfied with it. '... it isn't much good,' he wrote, 'but forms useful practice for later and more authentic attempts in the novel form.' He is probably correct in this judgment. The reader may tire quickly of the lengthy sequence of fantastic scenarios that take up much of the story. Nonetheless, some of the descriptions are masterly and undeniably charming.

As in 'The Silver Key' it is childhood that provides most happiness: 'Vaguely, it called up glimpses of a far-forgotten first youth, when wonder and pleasure lay in all the mystery of days, and dawn and dusk alike strode forth prophetic to the eager sound of lutes and song, unclosing fiery gates toward further and surprising marvels.'

At 43,000 words, it is his longest work of fiction to date and, combining horror and fantasy elements in a tale that illustrates humankind's ability to dream, represents a major achievement of this period of his life. It would be published in 1943 by August Derleth's Arkham House. It features Randolph Carter in a kind of modern odyssey, visiting strange places and encountering bizarre beings.

Building the Backdrop

There are also many connections to other Lovecraft stories. Richard Upton Pickman appears as a ghoul; the priest Atal has already appeared in 'The Cats of Ulthar' and will appear again in the 1933 story 'The Other Gods'; Nyarlothotep, the Crawling Chaos, is

Arthur Goodenough and Lovecraft outside Goodenough's house in West Brattleboro, Vermont, 1927.

often featured in Lovecraft's work, although this is the only time he actually interacts with a character; the dreamer, Kuranes, first appeared in the story 'Celephaïs'; the Plateau of Leng is referred to in 'The Hound' and will appear in *At the Mountains of Madness*; and Kadath will be mentioned in a quote from the *Necronomicon* in 1928's 'The Dunwich Horror'. So, it is possible to see how Lovecraft was carefully constructing a world that provides the backdrop to many of his stories.

Resurrecting the Dead

Finishing this lengthy piece of work, Lovecraft threw himself immediately into another even longer one, the 51,500-word *The Case of Charles Dexter Ward*. Written between January and March 1927, he never properly revised it in preparation for publication, fearing for its quality and marketability. He described it as 'a cumbrous, creaking bit of self-conscious antiquarianism'. It would first be published in the May and July editions of *Weird Tales*, and was in the 1943 Arkham House collection of Lovecraft's work, *Beyond the Wall of Sleep*.

The story may have originated from one that Lillian told him. 'So the Halsey house is haunted! Ugh! That's where Wild Tom Halsey kept live terrapins in the cellar – maybe it's their ghosts.' She is referring to the Thomas Lloyd Halsey house at 140 Prospect Street, Providence that some believed to be haunted. He may have taken the notion of a centuries-old man attaching itself to a contemporary person from Walter de la Mare's 1910 novel, *The Return*, possibly read by Lovecraft in the summer of 1926. At any rate, the characters of Ward and Curwen are both vivid and well-drawn.

But what makes the story so enticing is the way that Lovecraft has made Providence itself a central feature. There are a great many autobiographical sections such as 'the great westward sea of hazy roofs and domes and steeples and far hills which he saw one winter afternoon from that great railed embankment, all violet and mystic against a fevered, apocalyptic sunset of reds and golds and purples and curious greens.' The reference is to the railway embankment at Auburndale, Massachusetts.

Nowadays, *The Case of Charles Dexter Ward* is recognized as one of Lovecraft's finest works but he did nothing with it. It remained little more than a first draft. However, he was becoming increasingly aware that his best work was achieved when set against the background of his New England roots.

Spells of Terrific Screaming

'The Color Out of Space' was the last story of this productive period. Written in March 1927, it is one of Lovecraft's best works and was his own particular favorite.

This brilliantly told tale is undoubtedly one of Lovecraft's most terrifying. He is deliberately vague about the eponymous entity, creating horror on a scale that he had rarely, if ever, achieved before. He also succeeded in creating a truly alien being. He was disappointed with other writers' efforts to create alien life in their work, believing them to have too many human references. He strove to avoid a depiction 'of the human form – and the local human passions and conditions and standards ... as native to other worlds or other universes.' The entity in 'The Color Out of Space' is decisively beyond human experience and once again reminds us of Lovecraft's belief in the insignificance and powerlessness of humans in the face of the cosmos.

The story was eagerly snapped up by Hugo Gernsback's science fiction magazine, *Amazing Stories* that had launched in April 1926. *Amazing Stories* made a huge contribution to the recognition of science fiction as a significant new genre. Unfortunately, Gernsback paid a mere $25 for the story and even then only after three letters from Lovecraft demanding payment. He was left disillusioned and unwilling to write stories where he had not already been assured of publication.

THE CASE OF CHARLES DEXTER WARD

Charles Dexter Ward is a young man from a wealthy Rhode Island family who has disappeared from a mental hospital leaving only a great deal of dust behind. Ward had been incarcerated during a long period of insanity and physiological changes.

'... his organic processes shewed a certain queerness of proportion which nothing in medical experience can parallel. Respiration and heart action had a baffling lack of symmetry; the voice was lost, so that no sounds above a whisper were possible; digestion was incredibly prolonged and minimized, and neural reactions to standard stimuli bore no relation at all to anything heretofore recorded, either normal or pathological. The skin had a morbid chill and dryness, and the cellular structure of the tissue seemed exaggeratedly coarse and loosely knit. Even a large olive birthmark on the right hip had disappeared, whilst there had formed on the chest a very peculiar mole or blackish spot of which no trace existed before.'

A doctor, Marinus Bicknell Willett, investigating Ward's madness and the changes in his body, learns that for the past few years Ward has been trying to find the grave of an ancestor, Joseph Curwen, to whom history has ascribed a bad reputation. Curwen was a shipping magnate in the eighteenth century, but is also said to have dabbled in alchemy. He was actually a mass murderer who communicated with the dead. Willett discovers that Ward had found Curwen's ashes and, using magical formulae found in Curwen's house in Providence, had resurrected him. Curwen, Willett also learns, has killed Ward and taken his place. Unable, however, to fully fit into the modern world, he is declared insane and locked up.

Willett discovers a bungalow in Pawtuxet Village that Curwen had purchased as Ward. It is located on the site of Curwen's farm where 200 years previously, Curwen had indulged in his evil practices. Beneath it is a labyrinth where Willet experiences terrifying things:

'... Marinus Bicknell Willett was sorry that he looked again; for surgeon and veteran of the dissecting-room though he was, he has not been the same since. It is hard to explain just how a single sight of a tangible object with measureable dimensions could so shake and change a man; and we may only say that there is about certain outlines and entities a power of symbolism and suggestion which acts frightfully on a sensitive thinker's perspective and whispers terrible hints of obscure cosmic relationships and unnamable realities behind the protective illusions of common vision. In that second look Willett saw such an outline or entity, for during the next few instants he was undoubtedly as stark raving mad as any inmate of Dr Waite's private hospital.'

Willett learns how to return Curwen to the grave but also that he is involved in a global conspiracy with other necromancers to raise from the dead the wisest people who ever lived and gain through torture all of their knowledge, allowing the necromancers to take over the world. In Curwen's lab, Willett raises from death a being that is a mortal enemy of Curwen and his associates. Willett faints and wakes up back in the bungalow. The entrance to the catacomb has been sealed but there is a note from the being instructing him to kill Curwen.

Back at the hospital, Willett uses a spell on Curwen that invokes the deity Yog-Sothoth, that reduces him to dust. Meanwhile, the being has destroyed his co-conspirators.

The 1973 UK Panther Horror paperback edition. Cover art by Ian Miller.

THE COLOR OUT OF SPACE

The story is written in the first person by a Boston surveyor whose name we never discover. He is trying to find out why the people of Arkham stay away from an area known as the 'blasted heath'. He encounters an elderly man named Ammi Pierce who is believed by everyone to be mad. Pierce tells the narrator about a farmer, Nahum Gardner, who used to live on the property, claiming that it all began when a meteorite crashed there in June 1882. The meteorite remained hot and began shrinking.

Scientists who came to examine the meteorite were unable to discover where it had come from. As it shrank, it left globules of color that were impossible to describe: '... it was only by analogy that they called it color at all. When it is struck with a hammer it disappears.' That same night, the meteorite disappeared in a lightning storm. When it came to harvest time, Nahum's orchards were 'prospering as never before'. But disappointment followed.

'... with the ripening came sore disappointment; for of all that gorgeous array of specious lusciousness not one single jot was fit to eat. Into the fine flavor of the pears and apples had crept a stealthy bitterness and sickishness, so that even the smallest of bites induced a lasting disgust. It was the same with the melons and tomatoes, and Nahum sadly saw that his entire crop was lost.'

The meteorite had poisoned the soil and the problem continued, spreading to the vegetation around the fields, which became 'slightly luminous in the dark' and it began to affect the local wildlife. As the locals become concerned at what was happening, Nahum began to cut himself and his family off from the town, with Ammi Pierce his only contact with the outside world.

It affected his family badly: 'His wife now had spells of terrific screaming, and he and the boys were in a constant state of nervous tension.' As the vegetation began to crumble into grey powder, the water of the well became poisoned and one of Nahum's sons, Thaddeus, went mad after drinking from it. He and his mother were now locked in separate rooms in the attic but he eventually died. Nahum's other two sons disappeared. Pierce visited the farm and went to the attic:

'... He saw something dark in the corner, and upon seeing it more clearly he screamed outright. While he screamed he thought a momentary cloud eclipsed the window, and a second later he felt himself brushed as if by some hateful current of vapor. Strange colors danced before his eyes; and had not a present horror numbed him he would have thought of the globule in the meteor that the geologist's hammer had shattered, and of the morbid vegetation that had sprouted in the spring. As it was he thought only of the blasphemous monstrosity which confronted him, and which all too clearly had shared the nameless fate of young Thaddeus and the livestock. But the terrible thing about this horror was that it very slowly and perceptibly moved as it continued to crumble.'

He had descended to the kitchen, but Nahum had now been overtaken by the same fate as his wife. 'It had come to meet him, and it was still alive after a fashion. Whether it had crawled or whether it had been dragged by any external force, Ammi could not say; but the death had been at it.'

He asked the creature that had been Nahum – 'What was it, Nahum … ?' Nahum gasps:

'Nothin' ... nothin' ... the color ... it burns ... cold an' wet ... but it burns ... it lived in the well ... suckin' the life out of everything ... it must a' come in that stone ... pizened the whole place ... dun't know what it wants ... it beats down your mind an' then gits ye ... can't git away ... draws ye ... ye know summ'at's comin', but 'tain't no use ... an' it burns an' sucks ... it come from some place whar things ain't as they is here ... one o' them professors said so ... he was right ... look out, Ammi, it'll do suthin' more ... sucks the life out ...'

With that last gasp, Nahum 'completely caved in' and Pierce fled.

When Pierce returned with help, they found two skeletons at the bottom of the well, as well as those of other creatures. As they investigated the house, a light began to flood out of the well that became the 'color'. It covered everything in the vicinity and then, as the men fled, it shot up into the sky. Looking back, Pierce saw a small part of it fall back into the well.

Next day all that remained was Ammi's dead horse and acres of grey dust. The area had been abandoned ever since.

Interior illustration by Virgil Finlay for 'The Color Out Of Space' which appeared in the October 1941 issue of *Famous Fantastic Mysteries*.

PART 4
AT THE MOUNTAINS OF MADNESS

CHAPTER 10

THE DUNWICH HORROR

New Connections

By 1927, the UAPA had folded and amateur writing was just about over for Lovecraft. The last decade of his life would be spent writing to and helping to nurture the talent of a group of writers of weird tales, many of whom would go on to become important figures in the worlds of weird, mystery and science fiction.

One important new correspondent was August Derleth who first wrote to Lovecraft in July 1926. For the next ten and a half years they would write to each other, usually about once a week.

The first visitor to Providence in 1927 was Donald Wandrei (1908 – 1987) who hitchhiked from St Paul, Minnesota. Wandrei had ensured that Farnsworth Wright published 'The Call of Cthulhu' in *Weird Tales* by suggesting to him that Lovecraft would move on to pastures new if he did not. He and Lovecraft did the usual circuit of Providence and also visited Salem and Marblehead.

The Outsider and Other Stories

Meanwhile, there were various possibilities of a book of Lovecraft's short stories being published. J.C. Henneberger had suggested it in summer 1926, but nothing had come of that idea. Then Farnsworth Wright brought up the notion of a collection of his best work to-date. The project would be hanging around for several years but eventually nothing came of it. Worryingly, however, *Weird Tales* hit hard times with the onset of the Depression and was forced to adopt a bi-monthly

DONALD WANDREI

Wandrei was the son of the chief editor of West Publishing Company, a leading law publisher, and Donald was born in and would live all of his life in St Paul. He wrote short stories for his school newspaper and worked part-time at the St Paul Public Library. In 1928, he graduated from the University of Minnesota with a B.A. in English, having edited the university newspaper while there. At the time, he was greatly influenced by Arthur Machen's semi-autobiographical novel, *The Hill of Dreams*. Wandrei started writing in 1926 and his work could be found in the pulps until the late 1930s. He was also an accomplished poet and wrote a series of sonnets – *Sonnets of the Midnight Hours* – that were published in *Weird Tales*. This encouraged Lovecraft to write his own sonnet sequence, *Fungi from Yuggoth*. Wandrei contributed two stories to the 'Cthulhu Mythos' – 'The Fire Vampires' and 'The Tree-Men of M'Bwa'. He co-founded Arkham House with August Derleth and it would not be unfair to claim that he is better remembered for that now than for his writing.

Donald Wandrei, Lovecraft and Frank Belknap Long in New York, 1931.

AUGUST DERLETH

August Derleth, from Sauk City in Wisconsin, wrote his first fiction at the age of 13. All his money went on books and amongst the biggest influences on his writing were Ralph Waldo Emerson, Walt Whitman, Alexandre Dumas, Edgar Allan Poe, and Walter Scott. After numerous rejections, he finally sold a story – 'Bat's Belfry' – to *Weird Tales* at the age of 17. He studied for four years at the University of Wisconsin, graduating with a B.A. in 1930.

During his studies, he wrote constantly and also briefly edited *Mystic Magazine*. Returning home to Sauk City, he wrote horror stories that he sold to *Weird Tales* while working in a canning factory. He was awarded a Guggenheim Fellowship for his work on the *Sac Prairie Saga*, a series of writings about life in Wisconsin.

In 1939, Derleth co-founded Arkham House with another of Lovecraft's friends, Donald Wandrei with the aim of publishing the works of H.P. Lovecraft. In 1939, they published *The Outsider and Others*, a collection of most of Lovecraft's short stories. After publishing *Someone in the Dark*, a collection of Derleth's stories in 1941, Arkham House launched a regular publishing programme.

Derleth was also at this time teaching American Regional Literature at the University of Wisconsin and from 1941 to 1960, he was literary editor of *The Capital Times* newspaper in Madison. Meanwhile, he wrote a greatly admired series of seventy stories in an affectionate pastiche of Sherlock Holmes, featuring the British detective Solar Pons, and also wrote many children's books.

It was Derleth who coined the term 'Cthulhu Mythos' to describe the universe created by Lovecraft in his work. This was added to by other writers. Derleth began concocting stories from notes and fragments left by Lovecraft and calling himself a 'posthumous collaborator'. These appeared in *Weird Tales* and later as a book.

There has been discontent about this practice, with a number of people condemning Derleth as merely exploiting Lovecraft's name for his own benefit. Many, too, were unhappy with his use of the term 'Cthulhu Mythos' where Lovecraft used the term 'Yog-Sothothery'.

There is also a Christian world view in Derleth's collaborations that was alien to that of Lovecraft who was an atheist and championed the notion of an amoral universe. There is little doubt, however, that his founding of Arkham House has helped to rescue Lovecraft's literary reputation and provide him with a legacy.

schedule in order to keep afloat. A book of Lovecraft's work was not a priority.

In 1927, however, the project was still afloat and Lovecraft provided suggested contents – 'The Outsider', 'Arthur Jermyn', 'The Rats in the Walls', 'The Picture in the House', 'Pickman's Model', 'The Music of Erich Zann', 'Dagon', 'The Statement of Randolph Carter', and 'The Cats of Ulthar'. Lovecraft estimated this to amount to 32,400 words. The suggested 45,000 words would be completed with one of 'The Color Out of Space', 'The Call of Cthulhu' or 'The Horror at Red Hook'. He, naturally, would have preferred it to be 'The Color Out of Space'. His suggested title was *The Outsider and Other Stories*.

W. Paul Cook was keen to publish 'The Shunned House' as a chapbook of sixty pages in length. By spring of 1928 it was beginning to look like this book was going to happen.

Cook was chasing Lovecraft to read proofs and apparently, by the end of June 1928, three hundred copies of the book had been printed but not yet bound. Unfortunately, by this time, Cook was ill, having had a nervous breakdown, and his finances were not good. Cook's wife died and he had another, more serious breakdown. It began to look increasingly unlikely that 'The Shunned House' would be published. By Lovecraft's death in 1937, the project was still in limbo.

I am on Alien Soil,

In late April 1928, Lovecraft traveled reluctantly to New York to visit Sonia who was launching her own millinery business in Brooklyn. She had put $1,000 of her own money into the shop which opened on April 28. He was there for six weeks but spent much of that time carousing with the Kalem

Lovecraft with the Lee boys in West Guilford, Vermont, 1928.

Club members through the night hours, only bringing them back to Sonia's flat next morning as she was leaving for work. '... all I saw of Howard was during the few early morning hours when he would return from his jaunts with either Morton, Loveman, Kleiner, or with some or all of them. This lasted through the summer.'

Nonetheless, she was glad to see him. 'Late that spring,' she wrote, 'I invited Howard to come on a visit once more. He gladly accepted but as a visit, only. To me, even that crumb of his nearness was better than nothing.' She obviously still had feelings for him but his hatred of New York was too great for him to consider spending more time there.

Possibly his comfort with his bachelor existence in Providence also contributed to the brevity of his stay with his wife. 'I am on alien soil,' he wrote to August Derleth, 'circumstances having forced me to be in the N.Y. region for quite a spell. I don't welcome this sojourn, since I hate N.Y. like poison.'

However, he was slightly more charitable when writing to James Morton: 'The wife had to camp out here for quite a spell on account of business, and thought it only fair that I drop around for a while. Not having any snappy comeback, and wishing to avoid any domestick civil war, I played the pacifist ... and here I am.'

Meanwhile, when not sightseeing in the New York area, Lovecraft had teamed up with Frank Long in creating an agency for revision and editing. They placed an advert in *Weird Tales* but it failed to bring in any work.

The trip was more or less the last straw for Sonia. If she had seen it as a last-ditch attempt to save the marriage it was a manifest failure. The following year she persuaded Lovecraft to enter divorce proceedings.

Open Up the Gates to Yog-Sothoth

After his outpouring of great work between autumn 1926 and spring 1927, Lovecraft spent eighteen months without producing anything new. He filled his time with visits to acquaintances and correspondents in Massachusetts, Vermont and Washington DC and the remainder of the time he earned some cash from revising other writers' work.

He was never one to force a story, however, once saying: 'I never try to write stories, but I wait until a story wants to be written. Whenever I set out deliberately to write a tale, the result is flat and of inferior quality.'

The next story that wanted to be written turned up in August 1928. 'The Dunwich Horror' is one of Lovecraft's

Vrest Orton and Lovecraft in Vermont, 1928.

THE DUNWICH HORROR

Wilbur Whateley is born in the bleak and isolated town of Dunwich on Candlemas, 1913, son of a crazy, albino mother named Lavinia and an unknown father. Lavinia's father, known as 'Old Whateley', predicts not long after Wilbur's birth: 'Let me tell ye suthin' – some day yew folks'll hear a child o'Lavinny's a-callin' its father's name on the top o' Sentinel Hill!' Wilbur seems older than his age and by the age of 13 is almost seven feet tall and mature. He is educated too, reading the arcane books in his grandfather's library. But the local population, is afraid of him and dogs bark when he approaches, possibly because of the odor that emanates from him.

Meanwhile, he is being taught dark rituals by his grandfather. Old Whateley is all the time buying more cattle, but, mysteriously, the size of his herd never grows and those cattle he does have are seen to be afflicted by open wounds. When Old Whateley dies in 1924, he manages to gasp a message to his grandson, imploring him to read 'page 751 of the complete edition' so that he might learn how to 'open up the gates to Yog-Sothoth'.

In 1926, Lavinia vanishes and is never seen again. A year later, Wilbur ventures out of Dunwich for the first time, to consult 'the hideous *Necronomicon* of the mad Arab Abdul Alhazred in Olaus Wormius' Latin version, as printed in Spain in the seventeenth century,' the book Old Whateley had urged him to consult. Failing to obtain permission to take the volume out overnight both at Miskatonic and Harvard universities, he breaks into the library to steal it. There, he is attacked by a guard dog and killed. Whateley's remains are hideous:

> 'It was partly human, beyond a doubt, with very man-like hands and head, and the goatish, chinless face had the stamp of the Whateleys upon it. But the torso and lower parts of the body were teratologically fabulous, so that only generous clothing could ever have enabled it to walk on earth unchallenged or uneradicated.'

Back at the Whateley farm at the same time, a monstrous creature that the Whateleys seem to have been raising bursts out of the house, having been neglected for some time. A few days later, after noises have been heard at the Frye house, a group of men visit the place and find that 'there was no longer any house. It had caved in like an egg-shell, and amongst the ruins nothing living or dead could be discovered. Only a stench and a tarry stickiness. The Elmer Fryes had been erased from Dunwich.' More devastation follows. Meanwhile, Dr Henry Armitage, head librarian at Miskatonic University, who had refused to let Wilbur borrow the *Necronomicon* has been attempting to make sense of Wilbur's diary, written in some kind of code. Armitage becomes delirious:

> 'His wilder wanderings were very startling indeed, including frantic appeals that something in a boarded-up farmhouse be destroyed, and fantastic references to some plan for the extirpation of the entire human race and all animal and vegetable life from the earth by some terrible elder race of beings from another dimension. He would shout that the world was in danger, since the Elder Things wished to strip it and drag it away from the solar system and cosmos of matter into some other plane or phase of entity from which it had once fallen, vigintillions of aeons ago. At other times he would call for the dreaded Necronomicon and the Daemonolatreia of Remigius, in which he seemed hopeful of finding some formula to check the peril he conjured up.'

Armitage possesses an incantation that will send the creature back to the dimension from which it came. He also has a spray powder that will render it visible for a moment. Thus, the monster is made visible. Family member Curtis Whateley later provides a description:

> 'Oh, oh, my Gawd, that haff face – that haff face on top of it ... that face with the red eyes an' crinkly albino hair, an' no chin, like the Whateleys ... It was a octopus, centipede, spider kind o' thing, but they was a haff-shaped man's face on top of it, an' it looked like Wizard Whateley's, only it was yards an' yards acrost ... '

The monster, it transpires, is Wilbur Whateley's twin brother.

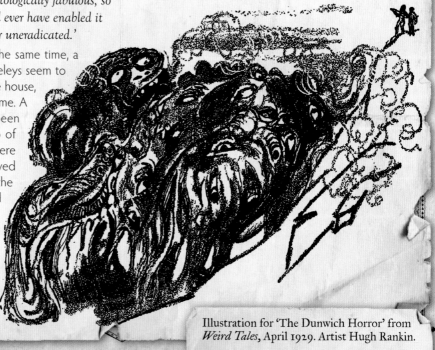

Illustration for 'The Dunwich Horror' from *Weird Tales*, April 1929. Artist Hugh Rankin.

IT'S EVIL BEYOND EXORCISM — AND THE SHOCK EXPERIENCE
OF YOUR LIFE BY AMERICA'S MASTER OF THE MACABRE

H.P. LOVECRAFT

INTRODUCTION BY AUGUST DER LETH

THE DUNWICH HORROR

AND OTHERS

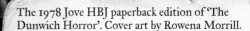

The 1978 Jove HBJ paperback edition of 'The
Dunwich Horror'. Cover art by Rowena Morrill.

core stories and one of the few in which the protagonists actually defeat the entity they are facing.

Lovecraft wrote to Derleth that the story 'takes place amongst the wild domed hills of the upper Miskatonic Valley, far northwest of Arkham and is based on several old New England legends – one of which I heard only last month during my sojourn in Wilbraham.' Wilbraham was east of Springfield and the story's Sentinel Hill is believed to be the Wilbraham Mountain.

Lovecraft was justifiably proud of 'The Dunwich Horror', describing it as 'so fiendish that Farnsworth Wright may not dare to print it.' He was wrong. Wright published it in April 1929, having paid Lovecraft $240 for it. It was the most that a single piece of Lovecraft fiction had earned to-date. It is a splendidly nasty story that builds in tension, horror and atmosphere towards a memorable climax and was the favorite of Lovecraft's works with a number of people including August Derleth and Lovecraft scholar, Robert M. Price.

Divorce

Lovecraft applied for a divorce on January 24, 1928. The grounds, agreed with Sonia beforehand, were her desertion of him. But, although he assured her that the divorce had been filed, he failed to sign the decree and, therefore, died a married man. This meant that when Sonia re-married a Los Angeles doctor in 1936, she was technically committing bigamy.

Lovecraft was undeniably upset by the way things had gone, believing it to be unbecoming of a gentleman to get divorced but he felt it only fair that Sonia be released from her obligation to him and allowed to get on with her life. The reasons for the failure of the marriage can be ascribed to all three parties involved in it – Lovecraft, Sonia and Lovecraft's aunts. Lovecraft was manifestly unsuited to marriage and once he was married, did little to make the union a success.

His involvement with the Kalem Club took up many hours that he could have been spending with his wife and he barely saw her from one day to the next while he was living in New York. One has to question whether Lovecraft was actually mature enough to enjoy a proper loving relationship with a woman, a situation probably arising from his upbringing.

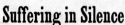

Suffering in Silence

Sonia's career undeniably got in the way of a successful marriage. She worked away a great deal of the time they were together and though they were ardent correspondents, it was no substitute for a loving relationship, although, as has been said, it is questionable whether Lovecraft was, in fact, capable of sustaining such a relationship. Sonia stipulated in her memoir of her time with Lovecraft, that she had suggested that they live in Providence and that they could purchase a property where they could live and in which she could pursue her business.

Lillian and Annie, however, would not countenance a female member of their family actually working for a living. '... the aunts gently but firmly informed me that neither they nor Howard could afford to have Howard's wife work for a living in Providence ... Pride preferred to suffer in silence; both theirs and mine.' Sonia's career would be social disaster for them and their nephew. It was the end of her attempt to change him: '... [I] had hoped to lift H.P. out of his abysmal depths of loneliness and psychic complexes.'

The last time Sonia saw Lovecraft was in March 1933 when she invited him to Hartford, Connecticut to join her in a tour of its colonial sights. Lovecraft became a distant memory to her and she would only learn of his death in 1945, eight years after he had passed away. After her second husband died in 1946, she spent her later years in Sunnydale, California where she died in 1972, aged 89.

25094/$1.50

H.P. LOVECRAFT
And Others

THE HORROR IN THE MUSEUM And Other Revisions

The 1976 Ballantine Books paperback edition of 'The Horror in the Museum'. Cover art by Murray Tinkelman.

CHAPTER 11

AT THE PEAK OF HIS POWERS

Back to Fiction

It took Lovecraft eighteen months to complete his next work of fiction. During that time, he had visited places that interested him, such as Vermont, Wilbraham and Virginia, in each place either lodging with acquaintances or taking a room in the cheapest boarding house in town.

He had also dropped in on old friends and had carried on writing phenomenal numbers of long letters to his seventy-five or so correspondents. Sometimes they were seventy pages in length. By this time, one of his regular correspondents was Robert E. Howard, creator of Conan the Barbarian and widely regarded as the progenitor of the 'sword and sorcery' sub-genre.

Lovecraftian from First to Last

Lovecraft was still receiving a small income from revision work and now and then he would try to find work but, of course, these efforts proved fruitless. As ever, the 'revisions' he did were more like full-length Lovecraft originals. He would sometimes receive no more than a rough plot and he would craft it into a tale. Zealia Bishop's 'The Mound' is a good example of that. Frank Belknap Long, acting as Ms Bishop's agent said of the final work: '... that brooding, sombre and magnificently atmospheric story is Lovecraftian from the first page to the last.'

But he was also suffering from depression at the large number of rejections he was receiving from both magazines and book publishers. Another writer might think nothing of making some changes to them

and merely re-submitting their work either to the publisher who had just rejected it or to someone else. But for the ultra-sensitive Lovecraft it was difficult to summon up the will-power to work in that way.

He was never any good at marketing himself or his work – it was not terribly gentlemanly, after all – and was by this time submitting mostly to amateur publications. He stayed away from national magazines and did not make any effort to help his situation by employing a literary agent. He felt that the commercial world of writing was out of reach for his type of work. '... there are probably seven persons, in all,' he wrote, 'who really like my work; and they are enough.'

He did write some interesting poetry during this hiatus – thirty-six 'psuedo-sonnets' – *Fungi from Yuggoth* – written between December 27, 1929 and January 4, 1930. Individual sonnets would appear in *Weird Tales* and in other magazines. He seems to have re-kindled his passion for versification while revising Maurice W. Moe's *Doorways to Poetry*, a critical history of verse. They are, in reality, not part of a single coherent work, the styles varying and a unifying idea being absent.

Venerated by a Cult

Finally, he turned his hand once more to fiction, in the form of the story 'The Whisperer in Darkness', a tale of science fiction and horror. The tale is notable for the introduction of the extraterrestrial race of fungoid beings, the Mi-Go. It was begun in spring and worked on throughout the summer of 1930, being completed in September.

ROBERT E. HOWARD

Howard was born in Texas, the son of a doctor. It was his mother who instilled in him a love of poetry and literature and who encouraged him to write and he began to write stories at the age of 9. These were mostly in the historical fiction genre featuring Arabs, Vikings, battles and lots of bloodshed.

His early writing was influenced by Jack London's stories and the work of Rudyard Kipling as well as the mythological tales of Thomas Bulfinch that had also made such an impact on the young H.P. Lovecraft. His family moved to Cross Plains, Texas where they would live until Howard's death. He discovered pulp magazines at the age of 15, and soon he was submitting his own stories to publications such as *Adventure* and *Argosy*.

None were accepted but he began to learn how to tailor his stories to specific markets. He finally sold a story about a caveman –'Spear and Fang' – to *Weird Tales* for $16 and shortly after, another, 'The Hyena', was also accepted. He dropped out of high school to become a professional writer, and was a regular contributor to *Weird Tales*.

In August 1929, his story 'The Shadow Kingdom', featuring the barbarian Kull, was published in *Weird Tales*, initiating the style known as 'sword and sorcery', a sub-genre that is characterized by sword-wielding heroes, romance, magic and the supernatural. In 1932, he conceived the character, Conan and invented a world for him – his Hyborian Age.

After appearing in *Weird Tales* for the first time in December 1932, Conan became so popular that a further seventeen stories appeared in the next three years. By 1936, Howard was devoting all his time to writing westerns but his life was falling apart. *Weird Tales* had fallen behind in its payments and his friends were leaving or getting married. Worst of all, his mother, who had suffered from tuberculosis for many years was dying.

On June 11, 1936, with his mother in a coma, he walked out to his car in the driveway of the family house, took a pistol out of the glovebox and shot himself through the head. He died eight hours later and his mother passed away the following day. His character Conan has become a pop-culture icon.

PEARL OF SEARCHING (1924)
BY NICHOLAS ROERICH (1874 – 1947)

Roerich was a Russian painter who was interested in hypnosis and other spiritual practices. In *At the Mountains of Madness*, Lovecraft mentions 'the strange and disturbing Asian paintings of Nicholas Roerich', and the paintings may have influenced Lovecraft's description of the icy desolation of an alien-haunted Antarctica.

Farnsworth Wright paid Lovecraft $350 for 'The Whisperer in Darkness', the largest cheque he would ever receive for a single story. It was going to be run as a two-part serial but it was in 1931 that economic circumstances forced *Weird Tales* into becoming a bi-monthly publication, a state of affairs that would last around six months. Therefore, the story was published complete in the issue of August 1931.

'The Whisperer in Darkness' is an excellent piece of work that has benefitted from Lovecraft's roaming before it was written, incorporating some vivid description of the Vermont landscape, as it does. The story was also subject to constructive criticism before completion by several of Lovecraft's circle, a process that undoubtedly made it a better piece of work.

Higher than the Himalayas

Between 1928 and 1930, Lovecraft had produced only two stories – 'The Dunwich Horror' and 'The Whisperer in Darkness'. He had also carried out three revisions for Zealia Bishop – 'The Mound', 'The Curse of Yig' and 'Medusa's Coil'. He had written some poetry and, of course, had written countless letters.

On February 24, 1931, he began his greatest work, the 40,000-word novella *At the Mountains of Madness*. He was delighted that Farnsworth Wright had published all of 'The Whisperer in Darkness' in one issue of *Weird Tales* and saw no reason why he should not do so again. Little did he know that the *Weird Tales* editor would reject this significant novella as 'unconvincing'.

It would not be until the March and April 1936 issues of *Astounding Tales* that *At the Mountains of Madness* would finally see the light of day. In this story Lovecraft creates a notion that has been borrowed on many occasions – from *The Thing* to *Alien* – the discovery of horror beyond imagining that has been in hibernation for millennia only to be awakened by the unwitting members of a scientific expedition.

Authentic Icy Magnificence

At the Mountains of Madness contains several cross-references with other Lovecraft stories. The shoggoths, for instance will appear in his 1931 story *The Shadow over Innsmouth*, 1933's 'The Thing on the Doorstep' and 'The Haunter of the Dark' of 1935. The Elder Things pop up in the 1933 story, 'The Dreams in the Witch House'. The sponsor of the expedition is the Nathaniel Derby Pickman Foundation; this combines the names of two Lovecraft characters – Richard Upton Pickman of 'Pickman's Model' and Edward Pickman Derby of 'The Thing on the Doorstep'. Cthulhu appears in several places in the story as does the sinking of the city of R'lyeh, the *Necronomicon* and Miskatonic University. Albert Wilmarth from 'The Whisperer in Darkness' is referenced several times.

There is an icy magnificence at the heart of *At the Mountains of Madness*. Lovecraft brings a wealth of scientific fact to it, giving it an authentic feel although some have found the scientific paragraphs – especially those in the first part of the story – a little excessive. As Lovecraft himself said: '... no weird story can truly produce terror unless it is devised with all the care and verisimilitude of an actual *hoax*.' And *At the Mountains of Madness*, after all, is presented as a scientific report.

The sheer scale of this story, its cosmic sweep and its cogent mapping out of millions of years of pre-human history would be enough to place it high on the list of Lovecraft's achievements. However, its build towards its epic conclusion and the harrowing encounter with the shoggoth itself make it unassailable in his canon.

Overlong and Uncommercial

Unfortunately, its publication did not go as its author planned. He imagined a two-part serial as with 'The Whisperer in Darkness' and believed the ideal place to split it to be right in the middle of the tale, after Chapter VI. In mid-June, after he had laboriously

THE WHISPERER IN DARKNESS

The story begins dramatically:

> 'Bear in mind closely that I did not see any actual visual horror at the end. To say that a mental shock was the cause of what I inferred – that last straw which sent me racing out of the lonely Akeley farmhouse and through the wild domed hills of Vermont in a commandeered motor at night – is to ignore the plainest facts of my final experience.'

The narrator is Albert Wilmarth, a folklorist and professor of English at Miskatonic University, who is investigating some strange events that followed the Vermont floods of 1927. There are newspaper reports of sightings of 'one or more very bizarre and disturbing objects in the surging waters that poured down from the unfrequented hills'. People began to 'connect these sights with a primitive, half-forgotten cycle of whispered legend which old people resurrected for the occasion.'

Wilmarth is skeptical, dismissing such people as '… merely romanticists who insisted on trying to transfer to real life the fantastic lore of lurking "little people" made popular by the "magnificent horror-fiction of Arthur Machen".'

Wilmarth receives a letter from Henry Wentworth Akeley who lives in a remote farmhouse near Townshend, Vermont in which Akeley claims to have 'certain evidence that monstrous things do indeed live in the woods on the high hills which nobody visits.' These creatures are responsible for the bodies seen floating in the rivers. They are, he claims, a race of extraterrestrial beings venerated by a cult that has been heard to chant the names of the gods Cthulhu and Nyarlathotep.

Akeley has actually made a recording of one of their ceremonies and sends it on a wax disc to Wilmarth. The two exchange letters but Akeley is attacked by members of the cult he has described, at which point he withdraws his claims, telling Wilmarth that he has met the extraterrestrials who are from the planet Yuggoth on the edge of our solar system and is convinced they mean no harm.

Wilmarth consents to returning all the letters and recordings that Akeley has sent him. He finds Akeley seated in a chair in his cabin in the dark. He explains to Wilmarth what the aliens have revealed to them, that they are able to surgically remove a brain and place it in a metal canister wherein it is able to 'withstand the rigors of deep space travel'. He shows Wilmarth the proof. Akeley informs Wilmarth that he has agreed to undergo this operation so that he can obtain knowledge that no man possesses. Wilmarth notices a canister with Akeley's name marked on it.

That night, Wilmarth overhears several voices conversing in another room and, increasingly uneasy, makes his escape in Akeley's car. When he returns the following day with the police, they find Akeley's dismembered head and hands that one of the aliens must have used, puppet-like, to pretend to him that Akeley was alive when he was speaking to him. They find Akeley's brain in the canister.

---

typed out all 115 pages, he was devastated to hear from Farnsworth Wright that the story had been rejected:

> 'Yes – Wright "explained" his rejection of the "Mountains of Madness" in almost the same language as that with which he "explained" other recent rejections to Long & Derleth. It was "too long", "not easily divisible into parts", "not convincing" – & so on. Just what he has said of other things of mine (except for length) – some of which he has ultimately accepted after many hesitations.'

Interestingly, however, Wright was not the only one who was not particularly fond of this story. Lovecraft's friend W. Paul Cook was not keen on the new direction of his work, the pseudo-scientific type of story, and others to whom he had circulated it were less than enthusiastic.

Wright, of course, had commercial reasons for rejecting work. His focus had to be on providing the readers of *Weird Tales* with stories they would enjoy and that would persuade them to keep buying the magazine and *At the Mountains of Madness* was a dense story, after all, replete with scientific information.

AT THE MOUNTAINS OF MADNESS

The story opens with Professor William Dyer of Miskatonic University relating his experiences during the 1930 – 31 Miskatonic Antarctic expedition in an attempt to persuade another heavily publicized scientific expedition not to venture into the same region. During his own expedition, he and his team discovered astonishing ruins and a range of mountains that are higher than the Himalayas. An advance party, led by Professor Lake, has crossed these mountains and discovered the remains of fourteen ancient life forms, barrel-shaped creatures. Lake relates his discoveries via a radio connection:

'Objects are eight feet long all over. Six-foot five-ridged barrel torso 3.5 feet central diameter, 1 foot end diameters. Dark grey, flexible, and infinitely tough. Seven-foot membraneous wings of same color, found folded, spread out of furrows between ridges. Wing framework tubular or glandular, of lighter grey, with orifices at wing tips. Spread wings have serrated edge. Around equator, one at central apex of each of the five vertical, stave-like ridges, are five systems of light grey flexible arms or tentacles found tightly folded to torso but expansible to maximum length of over 3 feet. Like arms of primitive crinoid. Single stalks 3 inches diameter branch after 6 inches into five sub-stalks, each of which branches after 8 inches into five small, tapering tentacles or tendrils, giving each stalk a total of 25 tentacles.'

They are non-human and seem to have evolved beyond anything found on earth. Lake has read the *Necronomicon* and suggests that these beings could be the Elder Things or Old Ones of which that book speaks. Radio contact with Lake is lost and Dyer takes several of his men in some small aircraft to find out what has happened. Arriving at Lake's camp, they find it devastated and all but one of their colleagues murdered. There is no sign of the Old Ones. There are, however, some damaged specimens buried in the snow which, they conclude, must have been the work of the one survivor of the advance party, Gedney.

Dyer and a member of the group, a graduate student named Danforth travel beyond the mountain range to see if they can find an answer. They discover a vast stone city, between fifty and a hundred miles wide, that had evidently been constructed millennia in the past.

As they explore it and examine the wall decorations and bas-reliefs that depict the history of an ancient civilization, they come to the conclusion that it was built by the Old Ones. They learn that the Old Ones came to earth from space around fifty million years ago and settled in the Antarctic before gradually colonizing other parts of the planet.

Their city had been built with the help of beings known as shoggoths, 'multicellular protoplasmic masses capable of molding their tissues into all sorts of temporary organs under hypnotic influence and thereby forming ideal slaves to perform the heavy work of the community.' Unfortunately, the shoggoths began to develop intelligence and had to be subjugated by the Old Ones.

Over the centuries, the Old Ones came up against other extraterrestrial entities such as the fungi from Yuggoth and the Cthulhu spawn that forced the Old Ones back to the settlement in the Antarctic that they had initially inhabited. They were unable to leave earth as they had lost the ability to fly and were forced to move to the ocean floor when threatened by an unnamed evil that lived beyond the mountains.

Dyer and Danforth are drawn towards a massive entrance that shields a tunnel that they believe will

Internal illustrations (above and facing) by Howard V. Brown for *At the Mountains of Madness* from *Astounding Stories*, February 1936.

lead them to a subterranean region described on the walls. They discover dead Old Ones and bizarre blind penguins, six feet in height that serve as livestock for whatever lives in this subterranean world. Suddenly, and horrifically, they encounter a shoggoth.

'... the nightmare plastic column of foetid black iridescence oozed tightly onward through its fifteen-foot sinus; gathering unholy speed and driving before it a spiral, re-thickening cloud of the pallid abyss-vapor. It was a terrible, indescribable thing vaster than any subway train – a shapeless congeries of protoplasmic bubbles, faintly self-luminous, and with myriads of temporary eyes forming and unforming as pustules of greenish light all over the tunnel-filling front that bore down upon us, crushing the frantic penguins and slithering over the glistening floor that it and its kind had swept so evilly free of all litter. Still came that eldritch, mocking cry – Tekeli-li! Tekeli-li!"

They manage to escape, but in the aircraft as they soar over the mountains, Danforth looks back and is driven insane by the horror that he sees. He refuses to tell anyone what he has seen and will never be the same again. Once again, Dyer implores the forthcoming expedition to think again:

'It is absolutely necessary, for the peace and safety of mankind, that some of earth's dark, dead corners and unplumbed depths be let alone; lest sleeping abnormalities wake to resurgent life, and blasphemously surviving nightmares squirm and splash out of their black lairs to newer and wider conquests.'

CONTENTS COPYRIGHTED 1936   FEBRUARY 1936

ASTOUNDING
STORIES
20¢

At the Mountains of Madness
by **H. P. LOVECRAFT**

The cover of *Astounding Stories*, February 1936,
featuring *At the Mountains of Madness*. Cover
art by Howard V. Brown.

Longshoremen and Coal-Heavers

Lovecraft was well aware of Wright's own pressures and did not think he was a stupid man, as he had written in 1927 to Donald Wandrei:

> 'Wright ... isn't such an ass as you'd think from his editorial dicta. He knows – at least, I assume that he knows – what junk he prints, but chooses it on the basis of its proved appeal to the brachycephalic longshoremen and coal-heavers who form his clientele & scrawl "fan letters" to the Eyrie with their stubby pencils & ruled five-cent pads. I think he works intelligently – as a sound business man – doing what he's paid to do, & steadily building up the magazine as a paying proposition.'

Eventually, *At the Mountains of Madness* was sold to *Astounding Stories* and serialized in three parts in its issues of February, March and April 1936.

Never-Ending Rejections

Lovecraft, however, must have been disappointed by the rejections he was receiving at this time. He had been approached in the spring of 1931 by an editor at the publishing house, G.P. Putnam's Sons, with a view to publishing a collection of his stories.

Lovecraft had sent thirty stories but a month after Farnsworth Wright's latest rejection, he had the same news from Putnam's. The reasons given were fairly ridiculous. Some of the stories, they said, were not subtle enough and that they were too 'uniformly macabre in mood to stand collected publication.' Lovecraft believed the uniformity of mood to be a strongpoint for a collection of fiction, but it was not to be.

The next rejection came from a new magazine, *Strange Tales*, launched in 1931. Lovecraft had submitted four stories all of which had already been rejected by Farnsworth Wright – 'The Doom that Came to Sarnath', 'The Nameless City', 'Beyond the Wall of Sleep' and 'Polaris'. And the following month 'In the Vault' was rejected. *Strange Tales* would last a mere seven issues.

Surging through the Spectral Moonlight

From the icy wastes of Antarctica, Lovecraft next returned to the familiar ground of New England. The 25,000-word, five-chapter novelette, *The Shadow Over Innsmouth*, was written in November and December 1931. It is an atmospheric story of degeneration, dubious ancestry, forbidden mystery and, of course, this being Lovecraft, things that are beyond the understanding of the human brain.

Farnsworth Wright rejected this brooding tale of degeneration and the dangers of miscegenation after it had been sent to him by August Derleth who believed it to be 'Lovecraft at his best'. For five and a half years after the rejection of *At the Mountains of Madness*, Lovecraft only once personally sent Wright a piece of fiction for consideration.

The Shadow Over Innsmouth appeared as a bound booklet in April 1936, the only work by Lovecraft that was published other than in a periodical.

Lovecraft in Brooklyn, 1931.

THE SHADOW OVER INNSMOUTH

In the first chapter, the narrator, Robert Olmstead, who is a 21 year-old student, is on a sightseeing tour of New England. He takes a bus to Arkham via the coastal town of Innsmouth which had fallen victim to rioting in the nineteenth century and is now so dilapidated that it is not even shown on maps of the region.

He learns that in 1846 a mysterious epidemic had killed more than half of the town's population. It was suggested that the epidemic might have had something to do with the voyages of a certain Captain Obed Marsh in the southern oceans where he had amassed a vast fortune in gold and jewels.

The narrator visits the Newburyport Historical Society where he sees on display a beautiful tiara that has come from Innsmouth. 'It clearly belonged to some settled technique of infinite maturity and perfection, yet that technique was utterly remote from any – Eastern or Western, ancient or modern – which I had ever heard or seen exemplified. It was as if the workmanship were that of another planet.'

Olmstead is curious and decides that he will spend the day in the town, catching the bus to Arkham the following day. As he arrives in Innsmouth, he notices how odd the people look, describing them as having 'the Innsmouth look':

'Listless-looking people working in barren gardens or digging clams on the fishy-smelling beach below, and groups of dirty, simian-visaged children playing around weed-grown doorsteps. Somehow these people seemed more disquieting than the dismal buildings, for almost every one had certain peculiarities of face and motions which I instinctively disliked without being able to define or comprehend them.'

He explores the town, finding it to be a place of moral and physical decay. He starts to feel depressed at what he sees and considers changing his plan and leaving early. He has been told the only person to ask about Innsmouth is the 96 year-old Zadok Allen but is warned that he is slightly mad.

Zadok spins him a crazy story about alien creatures that are half-fish and half-frog. He claims that Captain Obed Marsh had struck a bargain with these creatures – if they would give him gold, he would provide them with human sacrifices. All worked well for both parties until in 1846 the creatures began to mate with humans. There was uproar in the formerly normal and prosperous town and those who survived were forced to swear the Oath of Dagon, promising loyalty to the fish-frogs.

As humans mate with these creatures, they develop a kind of immortality and take on many of their features. They belong in the sea and actually can live in huge underwater cities for thousands of years. Zadok tells Olmstead he should get out of town at once because the locals have noticed them talking. But when Olmstead tries to board the evening bus, he finds it has engine trouble. He has to spend the night in Innsmouth at the Gilman House, the town's only hotel. It is not highly recommended:

'There was a factory inspector who stopped at the Gilman a couple of years ago, and he had a lot of unpleasant hints about the place. Seems they get a queer crowd there, for this fellow heard voices in other rooms – though most of 'em was empty – that gave him the shivers. It was foreign talk, he thought, but he said the bad thing about it was the kind of voice that sometimes spoke. It sounded so unnatural – slopping-like, he said – that he didn't dare undress and go to sleep. Just waited up and lit out the first thing in the morning. The talk went on most all night.'

Olmstead hears just such voices after checking into the hotel and feels a growing sense of dread and horror. After his doorknob is turned from the outside, he tries to flee but he is followed:

'I saw them in a limitless stream – flopping, hopping, croaking, bleating – surging inhumanly through the spectral moonlight in a grotesque, malignant saraband of fantastic nightmare. And some of them had tall tiaras of that nameless whitish-gold metal ... and some were strangely robed ... and one, who led the way, was clad in a ghoulishly humped black coat and striped trousers, and had a man's felt hat perched on the shapeless thing that answered for a head ...'

Olmstead escapes but later, after pursuing some genealogical research in Arkham and Boston, is horrified to learn that he is actually distantly related to the Marsh's family and has a cousin locked up in a madhouse in Canton.

He has strange dreams of swimming underwater and begins to fall apart. He even begins to take on the 'Innsmouth look'. He makes a decision:

'I shall plan my cousin's escape from that Canton madhouse, and together we shall go to marvel-shadowed Innsmouth. We shall swim out to that brooding reef in the sea and dive down through black abysses to Cyclopean and many-columned Y'ha-nthlei, and in that lair of the Deep Ones we shall dwell amidst wonder and glory for ever.'

THE SCREAM (1893)
BY EDVARD MUNCH (1863 – 1944)

Munch's most famous work, *The Scream* is one of the most recognizable paintings in all art. It has been widely interpreted as representing the universal anxiety of modern man. The 'screamer' personifies the 'Innsmouth Look' as described by Lovecraft – 'queer narrow heads with flat noses and bulgy, stary eyes'.

CHAPTER 12

THE WITCH HOUSE DREAMS

Summertime Travels

Around this time, Lovecraft began a correspondence with Robert Hayward Barlow (1918 – 1951). Barlow was passionate about pulp fiction and Lovecraft encouraged him in his first efforts at writing weird fiction. Barlow was an avid collector of pulp magazines and this passion for collecting would prove invaluable to Lovecraft's legacy in years to come. By 1932, he was typing Lovecraft's old stories. All he wanted in return were the original manuscripts. Lovecraft, who hated typing, was delighted. What Lovecraft did not know at the time was that the deceptively mature Barlow was, in fact, only 13 years old.

Lovecraft, as was becoming his habit, again spent the spring and summer of 1931 traveling. In May, he stopped off briefly in New York before taking a thirty-six hour bus ride to Charleston, South Carolina via Washington DC, Richmond, Virginia, Salem, Charlotte, North Carolina and Colombia, South Carolina. He moved on from there to Savannah, Jacksonville and finally to St Augustine, Florida, the oldest continuously inhabited city in the United States.

Towards the end of May, he dropped in on a new correspondent, Henry S. Whitehead in Dunedin, Florida. On June 10, he traveled south to Miami and the following day arrived at Key West. In early July 1931, he was back in New York, meeting with the gang, and on July 20, he was back in Providence.

His travels continued later in the year, although they were not as extensive as in the summer, mainly taking in his usual haunts of Salem, Marblehead and Boston with W. Paul Cook. They undoubtedly colored the writing of *The Shadow Over Innsmouth*, written in November and December 1931.

The Throne of Ultimate Chaos

In 1932, he began another story, 'The Dreams in the Witch House'. Lovecraft was depressed by the recent spate of rejections and the reaction to 'The Dreams in the Witch House' did not serve to improve his mood any.

Derleth had told him it was a poor story leading Lovecraft to respond on June 6, 1932:

> '... your reaction to my poor Dreams in the Witch House is, in kind, about what I expected – although I hardly thought the miserable mess was quite as bad as you found it ... The whole incident shows me that my fictional days are probably over.'

Totally discouraged, Lovecraft refused to submit the story to anyone and put it to one side. Around a year later, Derleth asked Lovecraft to see the story again and without its author's knowledge, submitted it to Farnsworth Wright who accepted it, paying Lovecraft $140. It was published in *Weird Tales* in July 1933.

Prolonging the Puppet Show

It must, indeed, have been a dispiriting time for Lovecraft. He seemed to be making little progress and his work still only appeared in *Weird Tales* alongside writing of the poorest quality. He wrote to E. Hoffmann Price: 'I dislike this trade because it bears a mocking external resemblance to the real literary composition which is the only thing (apart from ancestral traditions) I take seriously in life.' He saw himself writing in a certain way to please people like Farnsworth Wright. 'Every magazine trick and mannerism must be unlearned and banished,' he wrote, 'even from one's own subconsciousness before one can write seriously for educated mental adults.' He described his work to Clark Ashton Smith as 'a cheap, melodramatic puppet show.'

THE DREAMS IN THE WITCH HOUSE

A Miskatonic University mathematics student, Walter Gilman, is in Arkham, staying in the Witch House that is said to be haunted by Keziah Mason, a seventeenth century witch who vanished from jail in 1692 and who used to live there. In the last two hundred years, many of the house's inhabitants have been known to die prematurely.

Gilman begins to suffer from bizarre dreams and discovers that the strange shape of his room and the cryptograms he finds engraved on the walls permit him to travel to a dream world. In some, he encounters Brown Jenkin, a huge rat with human hands that is Keziah Mason's familiar.

In his classes at university, Gilman begins to display a brilliant understanding of the fourth dimension but his dreams are becoming ever more extreme. It appears that Keziah is trying to lead him on some kind of mission.

> '... when he awaked he could recall a croaking voice that persuaded and threatened. He must meet the Black Man, and go with them all to the throne of Azathoth at the center of ultimate Chaos. That was what she said. He must sign in his own blood the book of Azathoth and take a new secret name now that his independent delvings had gone so far.'

He spends his nights resisting the attacks of the witch. He is taken at one point to the city of the 'Elder Things', proving that he has been there by bringing back a miniature statue of an Elder Thing that he had broken off a balustrade in the city.

As things get worse, he dreams that he signs the 'Book of Azathoth' in the presence of the witch, her familiar and a 'Black Man' – the evil Nyarlathotep. He is taken to the Throne of Chaos and participates in the kidnapping of a baby. Next morning, he finds mud on his feet and there are reports in the newspaper of a baby being taken in the night.

On the last night of April – Walpurgis Night – Gilman has a dream in which the witch and Brown Jenkin are sacrificing the baby he had helped them kidnap. Gilman stops the bizarre ritual by strangling Keziah but Brown Jenkin manages to kill the child before escaping. Gilman is rendered deaf by an unearthly sound.

He recounts his story to a fellow boarder, Frank Elwood, who that night hears Gilman screaming and finds him dead: 'It would be barbarous to do more than suggest what had killed Gilman. There had been virtually a tunnel through his body – something had eaten his heart out.'

The house is abandoned and years later when it is being demolished, there are horrific discoveries:

> 'There were bones – badly crushed and splintered, but clearly recognizable as human – whose manifestly modern date conflicted puzzlingly with the remote period at which their only possible lurking-place, the low, slant-floored loft overhead, had supposedly been sealed from all human access. The coroner's physician decided that some belonged to a small child, while certain others – found mixed with shreds of rotten brownish cloth – belonged to a rather undersized, bent female of advanced years.'

The workmen also find the crushed skeleton of 'a huge, diseased rat' with certain 'abnormalities of form'.

Meeting E. Hoffmann Price

In 1932, Lovecraft went traveling again, leaving for New York on May 18. He spent a week in the usual company before taking an overnight bus to Washington and onwards to Knoxville, Chattanooga and Memphis, Tennessee. He then journeyed to Vicksburg and Natchez. Finally, in late May, he arrived in New Orleans which he loved. There, he met the pulp contributor, E. Hoffmann Price for the first time.

The two men met on June 12 and twenty-five and a half hours later were still talking. Price provided a description of Lovecraft at this point in his life:

> '... he carried himself with enough of a slouch to make me underestimate his height as well as the breadth of his shoulders. His face was thin and narrow, longish with long chin and jaw. He walked with a quick stride. His speech was quick and inclined to jerkiness. It was as though his body was hard put to it to keep up with the agility of his mind ...'

Losing Aunt Lillian

Lovecraft moved on to Mobile, Alabama, followed by Montgomery and Atlanta. At the end of June 1932, he was in Richmond, Virginia, and then Fredericksburg, Annapolis and Philadelphia. He returned to New York but was immediately summoned home by a telegram informing him that his Aunt Lillian was very ill. In fact, she was not expected to live and when he arrived late on July 1, she was already in a coma. She died two days later at the age of 76 without regaining consciousness.

Needless to say, the loss of his beloved aunt compounded the dejection he had recently been feeling. She had, after all, been a fixture in his life since he had returned from New York in 1926. After the funeral, therefore, on July 6, 1932, he took off, taking a ferry to Newport. He would do this several times that month, writing on a cliff overlooking the Atlantic.

Burnt Holes in a Blanket

In August 1932, he visited W. Paul Cook in Boston and then traveled north to Montreal and Quebec in Canada. As ever, Lovecraft lived frugally while on his travels and Cook was quite shocked by the sight of him when he returned:

> *'I have never before nor since seen such a sight. Folds of skin hanging from a skeleton. Eyes sunk in sockets like burnt holes in a blanket. Those delicate, sensitive artist's hands and fingers nothing but claws. The man was dead except for his nerves, on which he was functioning ... I was scared.'*

Cook immediately took Lovecraft for a meal. Nonetheless, from the trip came his longest piece of writing, 'A Description of the Town of Quebeck in New-France, Lately Added to His Britannick Majestie's Dominions'. This 130-page travelogue provides a brief history of the region and then in intricate detail describes the sights of the city.

66 College Street

No money had been coming in for some time now, forcing Lovecraft to vacate his room in Barnes Street, Providence in May 1933. With his Aunt Annie, he moved into a five-roomed apartment directly behind the John Hay Library at 66 College Street. It cost each about half of what they had been paying for their previous accommodation.

Lovecraft was especially delighted by the house's colonial style and the pleasant neighbourhood in which it was situated. He took two of the rooms that would serve as a bedroom and a study and there was also an attic storeroom that he could use. How much he loved the place can be seen from his letters of the time:

> *'The interior is as fascinating as the exterior – with colonial fireplaces, mantels & chimney cupboards, curving Georgian staircase, wide floor-boards, old-fashioned latches, small-paned windows, six-panel doors, rear wing with floor at different level (3 steps down), quaint attic stairs, &c. – just like the old houses open as museums. After admiring such all my life, I find something magical and dreamlike in the experience of actually living in one ... I keep half-expecting a museum guard to come around & kick me out at 5 o'clock closing time!'*

On June 14, Annie fell downstairs at College Street and broke her ankle, necessitating a four-week stay in hospital, an unplanned financial burden they could have done without. But Lovecraft visited her every day.

Six Bullets in My Best Friend's Head

Finally, after all the turmoil, Lovecraft settled down to write a new story – 'The Thing on the Doorstep' – between August 21 and 24, 1933.

Far from Lovecraft's best work, 'The Thing on the Doorstep' is poorly written and in places the author returns to his former verbosity. The premise of the tale is fairly obvious and it does not embody any of the cosmic elements that embolden his best work.

THE THING ON THE DOORSTEP

The narrator, Daniel Upton, has been accused of killing his best friend, Edward Pickman Derby but hopes this account will clear his name:

'It is true that I have sent six bullets through the head of my best friend, and yet I hope to shew by this statement that I am not his murderer. At first I shall be called a madman – madder than the man I shot in his cell at the Arkham Sanitarium. Later some of my readers will weigh each statement, correlate it with the known facts, and ask themselves how I could have believed otherwise than as I did after facing the evidence of that horror – that thing on the doorstep.'

Upton describes how Derby has always been fascinated by the weird, that 'at seven [he] was writing verse of a sombre, fantastic, almost morbid cast which astonished the tutors surrounding him.' Derby becomes a student at Miskatonic University and then becomes quite a well-known writer of stories and poems.

At the age of 38, he meets a 23 year-old Miskatonic student named Asenath Waite who is from the strange town of Innsmouth. She is reputed to have hypnotic powers and her late father, they say, was a magician.

Derby marries Asenath against the wishes of his father and they set up home in Arkham where they carry out occult experiments. Around this time, people notice changes in them. By nature, she is strong-willed and he is weak, but occasionally he is seen driving her car with a demonic expression on his face, even though he has never learned to drive. She, on the other hand, has been seen at a window, looking meek.

One day, Upton receives a phone call telling him that Derby is in a disturbed state in Maine. Having driven there, he now seems to have forgotten how to drive. Driving him back, Upton is told a strange story by his friend. Asenath has forced him out of his body, he claims, and is, in fact, Ephraim, her father who had placed his mind in his daughter's body as he died. Suddenly, however, Derby clams up and takes the wheel of the car, advising Upton to forget what he has just been told. A few months later Upton visits Derby, again finding him disturbed. Asenath, he tells him, has left him and wants a divorce.

At Christmas Derby has a breakdown and is admitted to a mental hospital. For some time he is ill but suddenly one day seems to have recovered. Upton is concerned, however, to find him in the same condition he was in during the car journey back from Maine.

'I saw in an instant that he bore the strangely energized personality which had seemed so foreign to his own nature – the competent personality I had found so vaguely horrible, and which Edward himself had once vowed was the intruding soul of his wife. There was the same blazing vision – so like Asenath's and old Ephraim's – and the same firm mouth; and when he spoke I could sense the same grim, pervasive irony in his voice – the deep irony so redolent of potential evil.'

Upton is very worried. Then, one evening he receives a telephone call but is unable to decipher what the caller is saying. 'I thought I heard a sort of half-liquid bubbling noise – "*glub … glub … glub*".'

Later, there is a knock at the door, the familiar knock that Derby always used. He opens it and 'for a second scarcely saw the dwarfed, humped figure on the steps. The summons had been Edward's, but who was this foul, stunted parody?' The creature, wearing one of Derby's old coats, hands Upton a piece of paper on which is written Derby's story. He has killed Asenath in order to free himself of her influence and to prevent her from switching bodies with him permanently.

However, the mind of Asenath/Ephraim has managed to escape and enter Derby's body, casting his mind into Asenath whose rotting corpse languishes in the cellar of their house. The 'thing on the doorstep' in front of Upton is Asenath, with Derby's mind, who has climbed out of her shallow grave to deliver this message to Upton. The note pleads with Upton to kill Derby. He goes at once to the mental hospital and fires six bullets into the skull of his best friend.

'What they finally found inside Edward's oddly assorted clothes was mostly liquescent horror. There were bones, too – and a crushed-in skull. Some dental work positively identified the skull as Asenath's.'

Lovecraft scholar, Peter Cannon, says that 'The Thing on the Doorstep' is one of 'the poorest of Lovecraft's later tales' and Lin Carter describes it as 'curiously minor and somehow unsatisfying ... a sordid little domestic tragedy ... wholly lacking in the sort of cosmic vision that makes Lovecraft's best stories so memorable.'

It was not published until the January 1937 issue of *Weird Tales*.

Lovecraft's Widening Circle

Lovecraft's correspondence circle was widening and beginning to include a number of teenagers – mostly boys – who viewed him as a writer of legendary status. The young friend who would become most successful was Robert Bloch (1917 – 94).

Writing in Lovecraft Mode

Meanwhile, Lovecraft's adult friends were making progress. Frank Belknap Long had moved from writing weird fiction to the more commercially viable science fiction, his work appearing in *Astounding Stories* and many other periodicals. A dream that Lovecraft had had in 1927 was incorporated almost verbatim in his story, 'The Horror from the Hills', that was serialized in *Weird Tales* in 1931.

Clark Ashton Smith was trying to make the same switch and his work began to appear in *Wonder Stories*, the revived *Astounding Stories* and *Amazing Detective Tales*. He self-published a collection of stories, *The Double Shadow and Other Fantasies* in 1933. By the 1930s, however, he had virtually stopped writing fiction, turning his hand to sculpture instead.

In 1931, Donald Wandrei published a second collection of his poetry entitled *Dark Odyssey*. He was also writing weird and science fiction stories that appeared in *Weird Tales, Astounding Stories, Argosy* and in the newly founded men's magazine, *Esquire*. He also wrote detective stories and a novel in the

weird style called *Dead Titans, Waken!* After a round of rejections, it appeared in 1948 as *The Web of Easter Island*.

Many were now working in a Lovecraft mode, borrowing his themes and characters but Lovecraft had turned against the world of the pulps. He wrote to one of his correspondents:

> '... the popular magazine world is essentially an underworld or caricature-imitation-world so far as writing is concerned. Absolutely nothing about it is worthy of mature consideration or permanent preservation. That is why I am so unwilling to make any 'concessions' to its standards, so much disposed to repudiate it entirely in an effort to achieve real aesthetic expression even on the humblest plane.'

From Florida to Nantucket

After Christmas 1933, Lovecraft was once again in New York, meeting up with his old friends and encountering some new ones, too. Writers such as A. Merritt of whose work Lovecraft had been very fond since reading 'The Moon Pool' in *All-Story* of June 1918.

Back in Providence, he received an invitation from the now 16 year-old Robert Barlow to his family's home in DeLand, Florida. Lovecraft arrived in DeLand on May 2, 1934. The Barlow family lived about thirteen miles from the town in a log house that had an adjoining lake.

He spent more than six weeks there before moving on to St Augustine, Charleston, Richmond, Fredericksburg, Washington and Richmond. He returned home three months after he had set out. In August 1934, he traveled some more with W. Paul Cook and Edward H. Cole and then paid a highly stimulating visit to Nantucket.

The amateur writing world returned to his life when he reluctantly accepted the chairmanship of NAPA's Bureau of the Critics. He managed to pass it on to someone else the following year but wrote some of the National Amateur Bureau of the Critic

ROBERT BLOCH

Sixteen year-old Robert Bloch wrote his first letter to Lovecraft in the spring of 1933 while he was living in Milwaukee. He had been an avid reader of *Weird Tales* from the age of 10. He always maintained how grateful he was to Lovecraft for the lengthy reply he made to a young fan's letter and the two would correspond until Lovecraft's death four years later.

Lovecraft enquired in his letter whether Bloch did any weird writing and Bloch sent him a couple of short pieces that the older writer praised and helpfully critiqued. 'A critic might complain that the coloring is laid on too thickly – too much *overt inculcation* of horror as opposed to the *subtle, gradual suggestion of concealed horror* which actually raises fear to its highest pitch.'

Needless to say, Bloch's early stories were heavily influenced by Lovecraft and after Lovecraft's death, Bloch continued to contribute to *Weird Tales*. A member of a writing group Bloch joined in 1935 offered him a copywriting job and this allowed him to write stories in the office when there was little work.

In the 1940s he published twenty-three stories featuring a humorous character, Lefty Feep and in 1944 was commissioned to write thirty-nine episodes of a radio show called *Stay Tuned for Terror*. August Derleth's Arkham House published a collection of Bloch's stories – *The Opener of the* Way – in 1945. His first novel was *The Scarf*, published in 1947 and three more followed in 1954. When *Weird Tales* went under in 1954, he continued writing for numerous other magazines such as *Amazing, The Magazine of Fantasy and Science Fiction* and *Fantastic Universe* while his thriller writing began to appear in publications such as *The Saint* and *Ellery Queen*.

In 1959, Bloch's best-known work, *Psycho* was published. He had very little to do with the film version that was directed by Alfred Hitchcock but the film would help to make him famous. This story was an example of Bloch's technique of using interior psychology to create horror. '… the real horror is not in the shadows,' he said, 'but in that twisted little world inside our own skulls.'

Throughout the 1970s and 1980s, he was an in-demand scriptwriter for film and television and continued to write novels. He died in 1994 at the age of 77.

columns from 1931 to 1935 and a few other amateur non-fiction pieces over the coming months.

The Dust of a Million Centuries

By the autumn of 1934, he had not written any fiction in almost a year. He was finding it difficult to get what was inside his head down on paper, as he had written to Clark Ashton Smith in December of the previous year: '... when I come to put anything on paper the chosen symbols seem forced, awkward, childish, exaggerated, & essentially inexpressive.' These problems led to him taking three months to write his next story, *The Shadow Out of Time*. He began it on November 10, 1934 and finished it on February 22, 1935.

It is very probable that this story was inspired partly by a 1933 film, *Berkeley Square*, especially as we know that Lovecraft had seen it four times late that year. It tells the story of a twentieth century man who merges his personality with that of an eighteenth century ancestor. He described the film as 'the most weirdly perfect embodiment of my own moods and pseudo-memories that I have ever seen – for all my life I have felt as if I might wake up out of this dream of an idiotic Victorian age and insane jazz age into the sane reality of 1760 or 1770 or 1780'.

Reaction to *The Shadow Out of Time* has been ecstatic. For Lin Carter it is Lovecraft's 'single greatest achievement in fiction' and author and critic, Ramsey Campbell (born 1946), describes it as 'awe-inspiring'.

Lovecraft, of course, was less than satisfied with it, mailing it to August Derleth without even bothering to make a copy for himself. The story was first published in *Astounding Stories* in June 1936.

Counting the Sestertii

Lovecraft was no longer even submitting stories to *Weird Tales*. 'I send nothing to WT now,' he had told Derleth. E. Hoffmann Price tried to get him to send 'The Thing on the Doorstep' to Farnsworth Wright but Lovecraft persistently refused to do so.

Meanwhile, people visited him in Providence, Robert Moe, son of Maurice W. Moe in early March 1935. Later that month Kenneth Sterling (1920 – 95) dropped in unannounced. He was a fan but even though he was only 15, he impressed Lovecraft. 'Damme if the little imp didn't talk like a man of 30 – correcting all the mistakes in the current science yarns, reeling off facts & figures a mile a minute, & displaying the taste & judgment of a veteran.' Over the next year, Sterling, whose family had recently moved to Providence, was a regular visitor.

Robert Moe was back at the end of April 1935. At the start of May, Lovecraft was in Boston visiting Edward H. Cole and managed to squeeze in a trip to his beloved Marblehead. But Lovecraft was planning another southern tour as Robert Barlow had invited him down to Florida once again. Lovecraft totted up his worldly wealth, which was not much, and reckoned he could afford it – 'Counting sestertii, & I think I can make it!'

Lovecraft at 66 College Street, Providence, 1935.

A movie poster for the science fiction/drama *Berkeley Square* (1933).

JUNE 1936

ASTOUNDING
STORIES

20¢

The Shadow
Out of Time

H. P. Lovecraft

Van Lorne,
...

Cover art by Howard V. Brown (1878
– 1945). Brown's cover for *Astounding
Stories*, June 1936, illustrating *The
Shadow Out of Time*, was judged by
American science fiction author Lester
del Rey to be 'one of the best paintings
of aliens of all time'. His charcoal
interior illustrations were much more
restrained than his cover work.

THE SHADOW OUT OF TIME

On May 14, 1908, Nathaniel Wingate Peaslee, a political economics professor at Miskatonic University, suffers a nervous breakdown while teaching. When he wakes up in hospital, he has amnesia and has to re-learn the use of his body. However, he finds he has developed:

> 'an inexplicable command of many almost unknown sorts of knowledge – a command which I seemed to wish to hide rather than display. I would inadvertently refer, with casual assurance, to specific events in dim ages outside of the range of accepted history – passing off such references as a jest when I saw the surprise they created. And I had a way of speaking of the future which two or three times caused actual fright.'

His life falls to pieces and his wife divorces him, only one of his children, Wingate, maintaining contact with him. But suddenly, on September 27, 1913, Peaslee becomes his old self, believing himself still to be teaching and that it is 1908. But he now suffers from bizarre dreams that he comes to believe are actually memories. He thinks that his mind has been placed in the head of an alien being 'whose head lay at the end of a flexible neck of enormous length. Retracting this neck and gazing down very sharply, I saw the scaly, rugose, iridescent bulk of a vast cone ten feet tall and ten feet wide at the base.'

Such creatures are part of the Great Race of Yith, an extraterrestrial species that possesses the ability to travel through space and time. They achieve this by switching bodies with hosts from the spatial or temporal destination they wish to be in. One hundred and fifty million years in the past the Great Race has established a colony in the Great Sandy Desert in Australia and at some point in the past they have occupied the bodies of cone-shaped beings.

They study the history of time and places and have collected a massive library city filled with the past and future history of many races, including humans. Peaslee contributes a history of his own times for the Great Race's library. Peaslee wonders if his dreams are no more than the result of his studies during his amnesia but he receives a letter from an Australian explorer, Robert B. F. Mackenzie, informing him that the archaeological remains he has described in his articles as the city of the Great Race have been discovered.

Peaslee accompanies Mackenzie to the ruins and finds that what he has seen in his dreams may be real. Leaving camp one night on his own, he wanders through the underground corridors of the city, realizing that it is all familiar. To prove it, he has to find the written account he has provided for the Great Race's library.

Eventually, he finds it and reads it, but on the way to the surface it is wrested from him by a great 'tumult of wind as I had never known before on our planet's surface'. Out in the sunlight at last, he says:

> 'I have said that the awful truth behind my tortured years of dreaming hinges absolutely upon the actuality of what I thought I saw in those Cyclopean, buried ruins. It has been hard for me, literally, to set down that crucial revelation, though no reader can have failed to guess it. Of course, it lay in that book within the metal case – the case which I pried out of its lair amidst the dust of a million centuries. No eye had seen, no hand had touched that book since the advent of man to this planet. And yet, when I flashed my torch upon it in that frightful abyss, I saw that the queerly pigmented letters on the brittle, aeon-browned cellulose pages were not indeed any nameless hieroglyphs of earth's youth. They were, instead, the letters of our familiar alphabet, spelling out the words of the English language in my own handwriting.'

'They spoke by the clicking or scraping of huge paws.' Howard V. Brown's interior illustration for *The Shadow Out of Time* in the June 1936 issue of *Astounding Stories*.

PART 5

THE HAUNTER OF THE DARK

CHAPTER 13

I AM PROVIDENCE

Two Cheques Arrive !

Lovecraft reached New York on June 5, 1935 but almost immediately caught a bus to Washington. He spent two nights on buses, thereby saving money on lodgings, and arrived in DeLand via Jacksonville on June 9. There he remained until August 18 and he finally made it home after passing through St Augustine, Charleston, Richmond, Washington, Philadelphia and New York.

In New York, Lovecraft had been introduced to an agent named Julius Schwartz who told him that F. Orlin Tremaine, editor of *Astounding Stories*, might be interested in any work that Lovecraft had. Lovecraft gave him *At the Mountains of Madness* and it was bought by Tremaine for $350. Then, in early November, Tremaine accepted *The Shadow Out of Time* which had been submitted by Donald Wandrei on Lovecraft's behalf, for $280. Lovecraft was astonished. 'I thought they had not the slightest shadow of a chance with Tremaine ... & I certainly wish such marketing could keep up!'

The two cheques arrived just in time. He had earned nothing from his fiction in 1934 and 1935 and had been in a parlous financial state – 'I was never closer to the breadline than this year,' he wrote. He was even having to be careful how much ink he was using, buying cheaper Woolworth's ink at 5 cents a bottle instead of his usual 25 cent Skrip ink.

A Blur in the Candleless Night

H.P. Lovecraft's last original story, 'The Haunter of the Dark', was begun on November 5, 1935 and completed four days later. It came about following the publication of Robert Bloch's story, 'The Shambler from the Stars', in *Weird Tales* in September 1935.

The Bloch story features a character who is never named but who is clearly based on Lovecraft. A reader had written in to *Weird Tales* and made a suggestion: '... why doesn't Mr. Lovecraft return the compliment, and dedicate a story to the author?' Lovecraft accepted the dare.

'The Haunter of the Dark' was published in the December 1936 issue of *Weird* Tales. Farnsworth Wright could hardly turn it down, after all, as a reader had suggested it. Robert Bloch actually wrote a third story in the sequence – 'The Shadow from the Steeple' – in 1950.

Headache, Nausea ... and What the Hell

Lovecraft visited with the New York gang at the end of 1935, leaving Providence on December 29, and returning home on January 7, 1936. During the trip, he was presented with a pamphlet printed by Barlow of his story, 'The Cats of Ulthar'. Forty copies of an ordinary edition were printed and two of a special one.

When he returned to Providence, Lovecraft complained of feeling unwell, putting it down to a bad case of what he described as 'grippe'. He was suffering from 'headache, nausea, weakness, drowsiness, bad digestion, and what the hell', as he put it. In spite of this, he worked on a collaboration with Kenneth Sterling – the science fiction tale, 'In the Walls of Eryx'. It was submitted to a number of the pulps but was finally printed by *Weird Tales* in October 1939.

Publishing Disaster

Just a month into 1936 and it was Annie's turn to be unwell. Suffering from breast cancer, she was taken to hospital where her right breast was removed. She then spent two

THE HAUNTER OF THE DARK

While in Providence to write, Robert Blake, a young weird fiction author, has been killed, possibly by lightning while sitting facing a window. The view in front of his dead body is towards the town's Italian district, Federal Hill. Blake had become curious about an abandoned church he could see and eventually decided to visit it.

Inside he found strange, forbidden books and in one room a metal box containing an odd gem or mineral that fascinated him. He also discovered the skeleton of an old newspaper reporter. He read the journalist's notebook and learned of the notorious Starry Wisdom church that was popular in the nineteenth century but, in 1877, suspected of being the site of satanic rituals, it had been shut down by the authorities. The notes also speak of a 'Shining Trapezohedron' and a 'Haunter of the Dark':

'Fr. O'Malley tells of devil-worship with box found in great Egyptian ruins – says they call up something that can't exist in light. Flees a little light, and banished by strong light. Then has to be summoned again. Probably got this from deathbed confession of Francis X. Feeney, who had joined Starry Wisdom in '49. These people say the Shining Trapezohedron shews them heaven & other worlds, & that the Haunter of the Dark tells them secrets in some way.'

There had been stories of something running amok in the belfry of the church and putting pillows at the windows to prevent light from penetrating. Then, on August 8 – 9, a huge electrical storm had caused a blackout that lasted for several hours. A crowd of superstitious Italians gathered outside the church in a candlelit vigil, sensing something enormous seeming to fly out of the belfry.

'Nothing definite could be seen in the candleless night, though some upward-looking spectators thought they glimpsed a great spreading blur of denser blackness against the inky sky – some thing like a formless cloud of smoke that shot with meteor-like speed toward the east.'

The remainder of the story is told from Blake's diary. He talks of terrible dreams and how one night he found himself fully dressed walking towards the church. He is obsessed by the fact that the thing in the belfry knows where to find him.

Then the diary details in staccato bursts how he feels he is losing control of himself as he sees a nameless thing approaching – 'I see it – coming here – hell – wind – titan blur – black wings – Yog-Sothoth save me – the three-lobed burning eye ...'

The following morning Blake is found electrocuted at his desk in front of the window which is closed and fastened.

Panther Horror
H. P. LOVECRAFT
The Haunter of the Dark
and other tales

The 1974 UK Panther Horror paperback edition. Cover art by Ian Miller.

weeks in a convalescent home. Lovecraft was effectively grounded while he looked after her as 'combined nurse, butler, & errand boy'. Naturally, the expense of all this was crippling to the already precarious Lovecraft finances. He was once again eating food cold out of cans, although this may have had more to do with his inability to cook.

Summer arrived late in 1936, but it gave Lovecraft the chance to get out, taking a boat trip to Newport on July 11, and writing on the cliffs that overlooked the Atlantic there. Maurice and Robert Moe visited later in the month and Robert Barlow turned up on July 28, staying for more than a month.

Later that year, Lovecraft saw for the first and only time a published book that bore his name. *The Shadow Over Innsmouth* was published by William L. Crawford. Lovecraft had recommended the artist Frank Utpatel to illustrate it and he provided four woodcuts. Unfortunately, however, the text was littered with errors, even after Lovecraft had laboriously proofread it. He was distressed when he received a copy in November 1936 and even corrected many copies of the book manually. It was a disaster.

The Last Grim Month

He spent Christmas 1936 with Annie who had now recovered and the two of them ate Christmas dinner at the boarding house next door to 66 College Street. The weather was mild and he had been able to go out walking in December and continued doing so into the New Year. But he was not well again – the 'grippe' was back.

He was really quite poorly, complaining to one correspondent: 'Am in constant pain, take only liquid food, and so bloated with gas that I can't lie down. Spend all time in chair propped with pillows, and can read or write only a few minutes at a time.'

His friend, Harry Brobst let Barlow know he was worried about Lovecraft: 'Our old friend is quite ill – and so I am writing this letter for him. He has seemed to grow progressively weaker the last few days.'

The last month of his life was grim and during it, he is thought to have kept a 'death diary' but it was lost sometime after Annie Gamwell gave it to Robert Barlow. The last piece of fiction Lovecraft ever worked on was a story called 'From

Lovecraft in the doorway of his home at 66 College Street, Providence, 1936.

the Sea' by amateur Duane W. Rimel that he was revising. The story was never published and is now lost.

Pain – Great Pain!

On February 16, 1937, Annie summoned Dr Cecil Calvert Dustin who deduced immediately that Lovecraft was suffering from terminal cancer of the small intestine as well as kidney disease. The doctor most probably prescribed painkillers, but Lovecraft's condition deteriorated and the painkillers were of little help. On another visit on February 27, the doctor told Lovecraft that his condition was terminal but the writer still maintained his optimism for his friends, letting them know only that he would be indisposed for an indeterminate period.

Annie asked Dr Dustin to bring in a specialist but there was little Dr William Leet could add to what Dustin had already diagnosed. On March 2, Lovecraft's diary bleakly records: 'pain – drowse – intense pain – rest – great pain.'

Patient and Philosophical

By March 9, 1937, Lovecraft was unable to eat or drink and when Dr Leet called on March 10, he recommended that he be admitted to Jane Brown Memorial Hospital. An ambulance transported him there that day. On March 11, Lovecraft's diary ends. On March 12 , Annie wrote to Robert Barlow:

'I have intended to write you a gay little letter, long since, but now I am writing a sad little letter telling you that Howard is so pitifully ill & weak ... the dear fellow grows weaker & weaker – nothing can be retained in his stomach ... Needless to say he has been pathetically patient & philosophical through it all.'

When Barlow received Annie's letter, he immediately telegraphed her from where he was in Leavenworth, Kansas, saying that he would like to come and help. But it was too late. Howard Phillips Lovecraft passed away at 7.15 on the morning of March 15, 1937. He was 46 years old.

I am Providence

Lovecraft's circle of friends did not hear of his death for several days – some, in fact, not for weeks – and, therefore, his funeral, held at noon on March 18, 1937, in the chapel of the Horace B. Knowles' Sons Funeral Home on Benefit Street, Providence, was attended only by his Aunt Annie and a small circle of acquaintances.

He was interred at Swan Point cemetery but his name appeared initially only on the central shaft of the Phillips' burial plot, below those of his father and mother. It would be forty years before fans would raise the money to provide him with a separate headstone inscribed with his name, his birth and death dates and the legend: *'I AM PROVIDENCE'*.

Peace Be to His Shade

The impact of his passing on his friends was devastating. Clark Ashton Smith, who had never actually met Lovecraft but had corresponded with him for fifteen years, wrote: 'The news of Lovecraft's death seems incredible and nightmarish, and I cannot adjust myself to it ... It saddens me as nothing has done since my mother's death.' There was a wave of letters in the amateur press and in the pulps from both colleagues and fans.

Farnsworth Wright with whom Lovecraft had endured so many spats, was touchingly respectful: 'We admired him for his great literary achievements, but we loved him for himself; for he was a courtly and noble gentleman, and a dear friend. Peace be to his shade.' For numerous people, Lovecraft had been an integral part of their lives for years. Many of them expressed regrets that they had not done more to help him during his lifetime.

Instructions In Case of Decease

On hearing of his friend and mentor's death, Robert Barlow had immediately jumped on a bus to Providence. The reason for his haste was that Lovecraft had written a document some months before his death entitled 'Instructions In Case of Decease', naming Barlow as his 'literary executor'. Of course, this document had no legal standing but Annie was anxious to ensure that her nephew's wishes were followed.

Barlow took away with him books and manuscripts, distributing as instructed by the document, some of the books to Lovecraft's friends. A week after the funeral, Annie had a contract drawn up that gave Barlow 3 percent of any sales of Lovecraft's material he made. In the years to come, however, he had neither the time nor the know-how to sell Lovecraft's stories. He initially deposited some of the papers at the John Hay Library of Brown University and a year or two later he donated the remainder.

The Stolen Archive

Library officials were not entirely happy to be recipients and these papers would only be catalogued thirty years later. They included all the manuscripts of Lovecraft's stories, apart from *The Shadow Out of Time*, his complete collection of *Weird Tales*, and a great deal more. It is to Barlow's eternal credit that he did this.

Unfortunately, some of Lovecraft's circle thought that Barlow had stolen the archive, the young man failing to inform them of the document the writer had left. Clark Ashton Smith, for one, was very put out, writing

Lovecraft and Maurice W. Moe, 1936.

to Barlow: 'Please do not write me or try to communicate with me in any way. I do not wish to see you or hear from you after your conduct in regard to the estate of a late beloved friend.' Donald Wandrei was also very upset with Barlow and remained angry with him until he died.

Some Turbulent Doings

August Derleth might, perhaps, have felt that he should have been Lovecraft's literary executor, especially as Lovecraft had written to him in 1932: 'Yes – come to think of it – I fear there might be some turbulent doings among an indiscriminately named board of literary heirs handling my posthumous junk! Maybe I'll dump all the work on you by naming you soul heir.' Lovecraft further wrote to him on this subject in late 1936: 'As for trying to float a volume of Grandpa's weird tales some day – naturally I shall have blessings rather than objections to offer, but I wouldn't advise the expenditure of too much time & energy on the project.'

Derleth was happy to take this as a green light for his overseeing of the publication of his friend's work and with Donald Wandrei's help, he devised a publishing program.

Three volumes of Lovecraft's work would be collected. The first would contain the most important stories; the second some poems and essays; the third a volume of letters. Derleth did this regardless of what Barlow thought, but ultimately Barlow assisted with putting together the manuscript that would ultimately become *The Outsider and Others*.

A Place in Literary History

To begin with it was rejected on account of its size, the cost of printing it and the fact that Lovecraft was relatively unknown by Scribner's, at the time Derleth's publishers. For the same reasons, Simon & Schuster rejected it. Derleth could, of course, have submitted a shorter version containing fewer stories, but instead, along with Donald Wandrei, formed Arkham House in order to publish the book. Its 1,268 copies, 550 pages, took four years to sell.

Nonetheless, it was well-reviewed, praised in publications such as the *New York Herald* and, naturally, the *Providence Journal* was full of praise. In the literary journal, *American Literature*, the pre-eminent Poe scholar, Thomas Ollive Mabbott (1898 – 1968) said of Lovecraft: 'Time will tell if his place be very high in our literary history; that he has a place seems certain.'

Beyond the Wall of Sleep

Meanwhile, Derleth was having more luck than Lovecraft ever had in placing stories with *Weird Tales*, but that was mainly because in 1940 Farnsworth Wright died and was replaced by Dorothy McIlwraith who more readily accepted Lovecraft's work. The only problem was that she published them in abridged forms. Thus did 'The Mound' appear in November 1940, *The Case of Charles Dexter Ward* in two installments in May and July 1941 and *The Shadow Over Innsmouth* in January 1942. Annie received almost $1,000 for these before she died of cancer on January 29, 1941.

In 1943, Arkham House published *Beyond the Wall of Sleep* in a print run of 1,217 copies. It featured two unpublished novels – *The Dream-Quest of Unknown Kadath* and *The Case of Charles Dexter Ward*. Again, the reviews were good. *Marginalia* appeared in 1944, a collection of stories, essays, biography and poetry. That same year, Bartholomew House obtained permission from Derleth to publish a paperback of five Lovecraft stories. 100,000 copies of *The Weird Shadow Over Innsmouth and Other Stories of the Supernatural* were printed. In 1945, *The Dunwich Horror*, another paperback containing three stories, followed.

Also in 1945, Derleth published the first of his posthumous 'collaborations' with Lovecraft, *The Lurker at the Threshold*, the first of sixteen such works. It marked the beginning of Derleth's promotion of the so-called Cthulhu Mythos.

SEPTEMBER

Weird Tales

25

H. P.
LOVE-
CRAFT

"Hallowe'en in a Suburb"

"...d of the Hands" — M...ARET ST. CLAIR

we'en in a Suburb

BY H. P. LOVECRAFT

HALLOWE'EN IN A SUBURB

The steeples are white in the wild moonlight,
    And the trees have a silver glare;
Past the chimneys high see the vampires fly,
    And the harpies of upper air,
    That flutter and laugh and stare.

For the village dead to the moon outspread
    Never shone in the sunset's gleam,
But grew out of the deep that the dead years keep
    Where the rivers of madness stream
    Down the gulfs to a pit of dream.

A chill wind blows through the rows of sheaves
    In the meadows that shimmer pale,
And comes to twine where the headstones shine
    And the ghouls of the churchyard wail
    For harvests that fly and fail.

Not a breath of the strange grey gods of change
    That tore from the past its own
Can quicken this hour, when a spectral power
    Spreads sleep o'er the cosmic throne,
    And looses the vast unknown.

So here again stretch the vale and plain
    That moons long-forgotten saw,
And the dead leap gay in the pallid ray,
    Sprung out of the tomb's black maw
    To shake all the world with awe.

And all that the morn shall greet forlorn,
    The ugliness and the pest
Of rows where thick rise the stones and brick,
    Shall some day be with the rest,
    And brood with the shades unblest.

Then wild in the dark let the lemurs bark,
    And the leprous spires ascend;
For new and old alike in the fold
    Of horror and death are penned,
    For the hounds of Time to rend.

H.P. Lovecraft (1926)

(Left) Cover art and interior illustration by
Virgil Finlay, *Weird Tales*, September 1952.

CHAPTER 14

THE CTHULHU MYTHOS

Robert Bloch's Shared World

Following the death of H.P. Lovecraft, the world that he created, took on a life of its own, subsuming the reputation and the work of the man who created the elements of which it was made up. A number of his contemporaries had already begun to write in the style of what would become known as the Cthulhu Mythos.

Robert Bloch, for instance, a long-time correspondent of Lovecraft, sent his stories to the older writer who became, as he did for many, a mentor of sorts. In particular, Bloch developed a fascination for the mythical books of the Mythos – fictional tomes such as *Mysteries of the Worm* by Ludvig Prinn and the *Cultes de Goules* by Comte d'Erlette.

Bloch's story 'The Shambler from the Stars' actually features Lovecraft himself. As with Frank Belknap Long's story of the previous year, 'The Space Eaters', in which Lovecraft also appears, he is killed off, something that seems to have disturbed Farnsworth Wright who insisted that Bloch obtained Lovecraft's permission for his fictional demise. Lovecraft characteristically authorized him 'to portray, murder, annihilate, disintegrate, transfigure, metamorphose, or otherwise manhandle the undersigned in the tale ...'

Borrowing the Demonology

The shared fictional universe of the Cthulhu Mythos was not, strictly speaking of H.P. Lovecraft's creation. Certainly, he was happy, during his lifetime, for contemporaries such as Clark Ashton Smith or Frank Belknap Long to borrow from his demonology or even to create stories from his ideas. He would, in return, borrow from them – Smith's toad-god Tsathoggua, for instance, appeared first in print in Lovecraft's 'The Whisperer in Darkness':

> '*I found myself faced by names and terms that I had heard elsewhere in the most hideous of connexions – Yuggoth, Great Cthulhu, Tsathoggua, Yog-Sothoth, R'lyeh, Nyarlathotep, Azathoth, Hastur, Yian, Leng, the Lake of Hali, Bethmoora, the Yellow Sign, L'mur-Kathulos, Bran, and the Magnum Innominandum ...*'

Derleth Builds the Myth

The man who really took Lovecraft's universe to heart, however, was August Derleth who had carried out an eleven-year correspondence with him, starting in 1926. In many ways, these two men were the exact opposites of each other. Lovecraft approached life as a gentleman displaying a frustrating reluctance to promote his work, regarding it as not quite the done thing. Derleth, however, was the model of the modern writer, pushy and confident, eager to get his work out to as many people as possible in whatever way he could.

Derleth was frustrated by Lovecraft's behavior, criticizing him as unprofessional and bemoaning the older writer's extreme sensitivity to rejection. It was Derleth who invented the notion of the Cthulhu Mythos, a pattern of myths throughout Lovecraft's stories that, to Derleth's mind, at any rate, made up a unified world. He coined the name after Lovecraft's death, Lovecraft never having used that description.

When Derleth had written to him on the subject, Lovecraft replied, describing it as 'Cthulhuism & Yog-Sothothery'. In fact, Derleth fashioned the Cthulhu Mythos in the way he wanted. He imbued it with Christian elements, namely that it was somehow a battle between 'good' and 'evil'. And, of course, good would win. He introduced his own deities – the Elder Gods – which represented 'good' against the 'evil' represented by Lovecraft's Old Ones and wrote stories that were based on this premise.

But, Lovecraft's vision of the Old Ones had nothing to do with good and evil. In fact, as we have seen, he was vehemently against human characteristics being ascribed to his creations:

> *'Now all my tales are based on the fundamental premise that common human laws and interests and emotions have no validity or significance in the cosmos-at-large. To me there is nothing but puerility in a tale in which the human form – and the local human passions and conditions and standards – are depicted as native to other worlds or other universes. To achieve the essence of real externality, whether of time or space or dimension, one must forget that such things as organic life, good and evil, love and hate, and all such local attributes of a negligible and temporary race called mankind, have any existence at all.'*

Posthumous Collaborations

Derleth wrote sixteen 'posthumous collaborations' with Lovecraft – published as written by 'H.P. Lovecraft and August Derleth' – based on fragments and notes for stories left by Lovecraft. Publishers were not interested and it was partly because of this lack of interest and in order to get these stories published that he founded Arkham House. Only a couple of them were accepted by magazines which is perhaps indicative of their quality.

In 1945, he 'completed' what he described as an unfinished novel by Lovecraft, *The Lurker at the Threshold*, but there was no 'unfinished novel'. Derleth merely took a couple of small fragments found in Lovecraft's notes that amounted to no more than 1,200 words. Many leading Lovecraft scholars are deeply dissatisfied with Derleth's posthumous collaborations, although others, such as Robert M. Price disagree: 'Derleth

was more optimistic than Lovecraft in his conception of the Mythos, but we are dealing with a difference more of degree than kind. There are indeed tales wherein Derleth's protagonists get off scot-free (like 'The Shadow in the Attic', 'Witches' Hollow', or 'The Shuttered Room'), but often the hero is doomed (e.g. 'The House in the Valley', 'The Peabody Heritage', 'Something in Wood'), as in Lovecraft. And it must be remembered that an occasional Lovecraftian hero does manage to overcome the odds, e.g. in 'The Horror in the Museum', 'The Shunned House', and *The Case of Charles Dexter Ward*.'

It is a debate that will continue, but what must be said is that without Derleth, Lovecraft's work might easily have slipped into even greater obscurity in the years following his death.

Re-appraisal for a New Generation

Derleth's version was accepted by critics, reviewers and other writers for some considerable time. It was only in the early 1970s that this approach to the Mythos became discredited after Lovecraft scholar, Richard L. Tierney, published a 500-word piece – 'The Derleth Mythos' – in a collection of essays about Lovecraft entitled simply *HPL*. It begins with the words: 'The "Cthulhu Mythos" is largely the invention of, not H.P. Lovecraft, but August Derleth.' Tierney then dismantles Derleth's notions of the Elder Gods versus the Old Ones and the idea of good and evil that Derleth introduced into his version of the Mythos.

It came at just the right moment, at a time when Lovecraft's work was being re-appraised by a new generation of critics and scholars. And when it was becoming extremely popular with a new generation of readers through the publication of paperback versions of Lovecraft's stories.

Ode to Lovecraft (2009). Fantasy art by Ania Bibulowicz *aka* CorporalPhantom.

CHAPTER 15

MODERN CONTRIBUTORS TO THE CTHULHU MYTHOS

Ramsey Campbell

One of the earliest contributors to the Cthulhu Mythos was the English author, Ramsey Campbell (born 1946) perhaps the greatest writer of horror fiction of his generation. At the age of just 18, the precocious Campbell's 1964 Arkham House collection, *The Inhabitants of the Lake and Less Welcome Tenants* (as J. Ramsey Campbell) impressed many in the Lovecraft community. He had first read Lovecraft at the age of 8 and had attempted his own Arthur Machen-influenced first novel aged 14. His first published tale – 'The Church in High Street' – appeared in the anthology *Dark Mind, Dark Heart*, edited by August Derleth. On Derleth's advice, Campbell re-located his stories from Massachusetts to England where he created the Gloucestershire city of Brichester that reflected his upbringing in Liverpool.

After briefly disowning Lovecraft in a magazine article, 'Lovecraft in Retrospect', he would later return to him, acknowledging his influence and publishing Cthulhu Mythos stories in *Cold Print* (1985). Whereas his earlier work could be described as pastiches of Lovecraft's work, these mature works were closer to homages. Of particular note are the stories 'The Voice on the Beach' and 'The Faces at Pine Dunes' in which a boy learns the horrific truth that his parents are involved with a witch-cult. His story, 'The Franklyn Paragraphs' is a bold Lovecraft parody, making an important contribution to the Mythos. This complex tale with multiple narrators, unspeakable horror and a build-up to a horrific crescendo is perhaps the culmination of Campbell's Lovecraftian work.

Colin Wilson

Another young British author would also make a significant contribution to the Cthulhu Mythos. Like Lovecraft, Colin Wilson (1931 – 2013) was fascinated by science from an early age and, by the time he was 14, he had written a book of essays on scientific matters entitled *A Manual of General Science*.

In 1956, at the age of 24, he published 'The Outsider', a study of the outsider in literature that became a bestseller. He was viewed as one of the group of writers known as the Angry Young Men that included writers such as playwright John Osborne.

In another work, *The Strength to Dream: Literature and the Imagination*, Wilson rails against Lovecraft, describing him as a 'bad writer', calling his work 'sick' and accusing him of having 'rejected reality'. August Derleth was furious when he read Wilson's comments and dared him to try to write a piece of fiction in the Lovecraft style. Wilson responded with *The Mind Parasites*, published by Arkham House in 1967.

By this time, he had warmed to Lovecraft and in his introduction to the book he writes that Lovecraft 'far more than Hemingway or Faulkner, or even Kafka, is a symbol of the outsider-artist in the 20th century'.

The Return of the Lloigor was a novella written by Wilson for Arkham House's 1969 Derleth-edited *Tales of the Cthulhu Mythos* that has distinct roots in the Cthulhu universe. The main character works on the real-life, fifteenth century book, the *Voynich Manuscript* that is written in an unknown writing system. Although it has been studied by many experts, including codebreakers, no one has ever been able to decipher the text.

THE MIND PARASITES
BY COLIN WILSON

This work tells the story of Professor Gilbert Austin's struggles with the Tsathogguans (Clark Ashton Smith's creatures also mentioned by Lovecraft). Invisible mind parasites that threaten the world's most brilliant people and the future of the planet. They can be defeated only by the mind itself, pushed to its very limits. Wilson harnesses Lovecraft's doomed vision and adds to it his own revolutionary philosophy to create a harrowing and imaginative page-turner. Lovecraft makes an appearance in the novel's early pages, when Austin talks of his writing and uses it to develop a theory as to how he can defeat the mind parasite:

> 'The study of Lovecraft was, in itself, an interesting and pleasant occupation. He was a man of remarkable imagination. Reading his works in chronological order, we observed a gradual change of viewpoint. The early stories tend to have a New England background, and deal with a fictional county [sic] called Arkham, with wild hills and sinister valleys The inhabitants of Arkham seem to be mostly weird degenerates with a taste for forbidden pleasures and the conjuration of demons. Inevitably, a large number of them come to a violent end. But, gradually, there is a change in Lovecraft's work. His imagination turns from the horrible to the awe-inspiring, to visions of tremendous aeons of time, of giant cities, of the conflict of monstrous and superhuman races. Except that he continues to write in the language of horror stories – no doubt with his market in mind – he might be considered one of the earliest and best exponents of science fiction. It was mostly from his latter 'science fiction period' that we were concerned ...'

This passage by Wilson shows a clear understanding of the evolution of Lovecraft's work and proves Wilson to be one of the few Cthulhu Mythos writers to fully comprehend Lovecraft's philosophy and the universe he created.

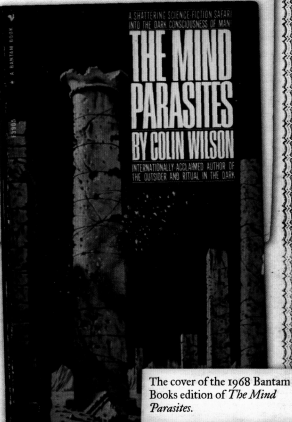

The cover of the 1968 Bantam Books edition of *The Mind Parasites*.

Wilson's character discovers that it is actually a medieval Arabic version of Lovecraft's *Necronomicon*.

The Lloigor of the title are a race of extraterrestrial pessimists from the Andromeda Nebula that wreak havoc on the earth every now and then. The human race is little more than an error and the world really belongs to the Lloigor.

Wilson wrote two other Lovecraftian novels – *The Space Vampires* and *The Philosopher's Stone*.

The Space Vampires, which was filmed as *Lifeforce* in 1985 by the *The Texas Chainsaw Massacre* director, Tobe Hooper, is about aliens who are brought to earth and suck the life out of people. They also have the power to project their minds into other bodies, an idea that might have come from Lovecraft's *The Shadow Out of Time*. The aliens, it transpires, are members of the 'Ubbo-Sathla', a race that had appeared in a story by Clark Ashton Smith published in *Tales of the Cthulhu Mythos*.

THE PHILOSOPHER'S STONE
BY COLIN WILSON

Howard Lester and Henry Littleway discover that transplanting a piece of metal alloy into the prefrontal cortex can produce a higher state of consciousness in an individual. They implant the alloy into their own brains and find they have a time vision that allows them to tap into racial memories. They realize that there have been times in the past that have been hidden to humankind by more powerful and intelligent beings.

As Lester says: 'I knew with certainty that there is something in the world's prehistory that cannot be found in any of the books on the past & it was obscurely connected with a sense of evil.' The book ends with a long account of the fall of the Old Ones but the question remains – when will they awake from their million-year slumber and what will they do when they wake?

Lester concludes that the human mind must evolve if the Old Ones are to be reined in, tying in with Wilson's own philosophy that the mind needs to be developed to a much higher level if humankind is to survive.

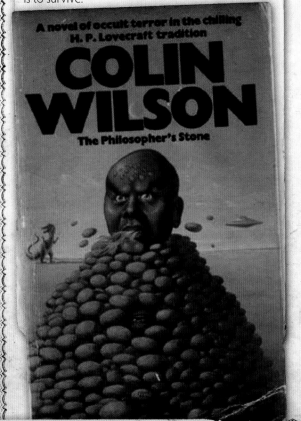

A novel of occult terror in the chilling H. P. Lovecraft tradition

COLIN WILSON
The Philosopher's Stone

The cover of the 1974 Panther paperback edition of *The Philosopher's Stone*.

Of far greater substance is *The Philosopher's Stone*, published in 1969, and suggested by Lin Carter to be more of a Cthulhu Mythos novel than *The Mind Parasites*, the action taking place almost entirely in the minds of the protagonists.

S.T. Joshi says of this novel; 'Much more so than *The Mind Parasites*, it utilizes Lovecraft's conceptions in such a way as to express Wilson's (not Lovecraft's) philosophical outlook. In this sense, it is one of the finest homages Lovecraft has ever received.'

Stephen King

No mean horror writer himself, of course, Stephen King (born 1947) has described H.P. Lovecraft as the twentieth century's greatest practitioner of the classic horror tale. In his semi-autobiographical book, *Danse Macabre*, he ascribes his fascination with horror and the macabre to Lovecraft's writing and cites him as the biggest single influence on his work. In fact, King is still fascinated by Lovecraft. His 2014 novel *Revival*, is dedicated to what he calls 'some of the people who built my house' – Mary Shelley, Bram Stoker and H.P. Lovecraft.

He said in an interview about the novel: 'I wanted to use Lovecraft's Cthulhu Mythos, but in a new fashion, if I could, stripping away Lovecraft's high-flown language.' In fact, King has written a number of stories in a Lovecraftian vein, including 'I am the Doorway' and 'Jerusalem's Lot' in *Night Shift* (1978); 'The Mist' and 'Mrs Todd's Shortcut' in *Skeleton Crew* (1985); 'Crouch End' in *Nightmares and Dreamscapes* (1993) as well as in Arkham House's 1980 collection, *New Tales of the Cthulhu Mythos*; 'N' in *Just After Sunset* (2008); the novel *From a Buick 8* (2002); and the novella written with Joe Hill, *In the Tall Grass*.

Jorge Luis Borges

Like Colin Wilson, the great Argentinean writer, Jorge Luis Borges (1899–1986), began by dismissing Lovecraft's work, but ended up imitating him. Borges did it in a short story in his collection, *The Book of Sand*. The story, 'There are More Things', carries the dedication 'In Memory of H.P. Lovecraft'. Even the title has a Lovecraftian bent, being taken from Hamlet's lines, 'There are more things in heaven and earth, Horatio, Than are dreamt of in your philosophy'.

Clive Barker

The English writer, film director and visual artist, Clive Barker (born 1952) works across many different media and has spoken of Lovecraft's influence on his work. He shares Lovecraft's view of the insignificance of humankind in the cosmos – as shown in his best-known work, *Hellraiser* – but his monsters breach Lovecraft's rules, being humanoid in looks and behavior and he rarely, if ever, uses Lovecraft motifs.

His short story, 'The Skins of the Fathers' features a man named Davidson who is stranded in Arizona when his car breaks down. He sees a group of bizarre monsters who, it transpires, have mated with a woman in a nearby town a number of years previously and have returned to reclaim the child that was born then. In the town, however, Davidson finds the inhabitants ready to kill the monsters when they arrive. It ends in disaster and Davidson and the few survivors end up sinking in quicksand and left for dead in the heat of the desert.

Neil Gaiman

The hugely popular fantasy author and graphic novelist, Neil Gaiman (born 1960) is a big fan of Lovecraft and has made a number of contributions to the Cthulhu Mythos. His Hugo Award-winning short story, 'A Study in Emerald' is a pastiche of the Sherlock Holmes story 'A Study in Scarlet' and first

JERUSALEM'S LOT
BY STEPHEN KING

The story takes place in New England in an unnamed town. Charles Boone has moved into the house that had been owned by his late cousin and becomes intrigued by the nearby deserted village of Jerusalem's Lot. When he investigates he finds that the church is full of satanic material. Amongst it is a copy of the book *De Vermis Mysteriis*. This fictional grimoire – also known as *Mysteries of the Worm* – first appeared in Robert Bloch's story, 'The Shambler from the Stars'.

His ancestor, Philip Boone had obtained this copy of the book in 1789. Charles discovers a huge worm under the church and just as in Bloch's story where reading from the book invokes an unimaginable horror, his touching of the book has brought the monstrous worm to life. This is something of a re-working of Lovecraft's 'The Haunter of the Dark' in which Robert Blake's closing of the Shining Trapezohedron releases the Haunter of the Dark, an avatar of Nyarlathotep.

Author Stephen King.

THERE ARE MORE THINGS
BY JORGE LUIS BORGES

While in Austin, Texas, the main character of the story learns that his uncle Edwin Arnett has died in Lomas de Zamora in Argentina. The dead man's house is purchased by Max Preetorius who sells off all the contents and begins to make changes to the house. In this he is opposed by the house's original architect, Alexander Muir. Bizarrely, the changes to the building are all undertaken during the night with windows and doors closed. All the nearby trees are chopped down.

The protagonist travels to Lomas de Zamora to investigate these puzzling events. He learns that the people of the town make every effort not to walk past the house, one of them telling him that one night, he 'saw something'. There are reports of a missing dog being discovered mutilated and decapitated on the lawn of the house.

The protagonist is forced during a terrible storm to seek shelter in the house. Finding the front door open, he senses 'a sweet, sickening smell' inside and switches on the light to discover bizarre pieces of furniture such as a long U-shaped desk that has circular holes at each end and there is an odd ladder that has irregular holes on each of its rungs. When the rain eases off, he decides to leave but as he heads for the door he hears the owner of the house moving in front of him. His curiosity gets the better of him:

'I felt that I had intruded, uninvited, into chaos. Outside the rain had stopped. I looked at my watch and saw with astonishment that it was almost two A.M. I left the light on and began cautiously to climb back down the ladder. Climbing down what I had once climbed up was not impossible – climbing down before the inhabitant came back. I conjectured that it hadn't locked the front door and the gate because it hadn't known how. My feet were just touching the next to last rung when I heard something coming up the ramp – something heavy and slow and plural. Curiosity got the better of fear, and I did not close my eyes.'

appeared in the fascinating *Shadows Over Baker Street,* a 2003 collection of stories that merges the worlds of H.P. Lovecraft and Arthur Conan Doyle.

The collection features Lovecraft's Old Ones as well as the main characters from the world of Sherlock Holmes. Gaiman has also written the darkly humorous short story, 'I, Cthulhu', in which Cthulhu is dictating his autobiography to his human slave, Whateley:

'I was spawned uncounted aeons ago, in the dark mists of Khhaa'yngnaiih (no, of course I don't know how to spell it. Write it as it sounds), of nameless nightmare parents, under a gibbous moon. It wasn't the moon of this planet, of course, it was a real moon. On some nights it filled over half the sky and as it rose you could watch the crimson blood drip and trickle down its bloated face, staining it red, until at its height it bathed the swamps and towers in a gory dead red light. Those were the days.'

Jorge Luis Borges.

Gaiman has said of Lovecraft: 'As a boy, I didn't think Lovecraft was a top flight author in his early stories. Once he got to stories like 'The Call of Cthulhu' it seemed as if he had found his voice ... much of his earlier stuff seemed to want to be Clark Ashton Smith or Lord Dunsany.'

Terry Pratchett

Terry Pratchett, (1948 – 2015) author of the *Discworld* series, has been known to parody Lovecraft's deities in his works, referring to them as beings from the 'Dungeon Dimensions'. In his *Moving Pictures*, the entity 'Tshup Aklathep, Infernal Star Toad with A Million Young' kills its victims by showing them pictures of its children until their brains implode. His Lovecraftian references are, like most of his work, humorous and entertaining.

Other Contemporary Writers

Adding to the Cthulhu Mythos is the Mexican writer, Luis G. Abbadie, an acknowledged expert on the *Necronomicon*. He wrote *El Necronomicon: un comentario* (2000) which collected his work up until that time. His most recent work is the novel *2012: El código secreto del Necronomicón*.

American writer and illustrator, Gary Myers, has written several books in the Cthulhu Mythos genre and the work of the self-styled 'Queen of Eldritch Horror', Seattle-based transvestite, W.H. Pugmire, often pays homage to Lovecraft's world. He has been described as 'perhaps the leading Lovecraftian author writing today.' His fictional location, the Sesqua Valley in the Pacific Northwest, is home to weird goings-on in a number of his books.

Others include Graham Masterton whose book, *The Wells of Hell* (1988) and *Prey* (1992) are based on Lovecraft's 'The Color Out of Space' and 'The Dreams in the Witch House' respectively; and British author Davis J. Rodger has created several new Old Ones in his novels *Edge*, *Dog Eat Dog* and *Living in Flames*.

Finally, there are countless anthologies out there of Cthulhu Mythos stories with all the above authors and many more. 2011's *New Cthulhu: The Recent Weird* features stories written by Neil Gaiman, Caitlin R. Kiernan, Sarah Monette, Kim Newman, China Miéville, Cherie Priest, Michael Marshall Smith, David Barr Kirtley, Lon Prater and Charles Stross.

Terry Pratchett and Neil Gaiman, 1990.

Die, Monster, Die, movie poster from 1965.

The Dunwich Horror, movie poster from 1970.

CHAPTER 16

STAR OF STAGE & SILVER SCREEN

Lovecraft at the Cinema

The cinema screen is the perfect place for Lovecraft's eldritch horrors and one must hope that digital technology will make the transference of Lovecraft's stories to the big screen easier and more affordable. It is to be hoped, therefore, that there will be more Lovecraft-themed films coming to a cinema near you. But there have already been a few, admittedly not Academy Award-winners, but interesting all the same.

The noted American independent film producer and director, Roger Corman made a film called *The Haunted Palace* in 1963 that was based on Lovecraft's *The Case of Charles Dexter Ward*. Even with those masters of the horror genre, Vincent Price and Lon Chaney Jr this story of a village in the grip of a dead necromancer, failed to excite. Confusingly, the title is taken from a poem by Edgar Allan Poe, the story of which was later incorporated into Poe's short story 'The Fall of the House of Usher'.

Two years later, another doyen of horror, Boris Karloff, tried to make sense of a mediocre script in a movie entitled *Monster of Terror* (*Die, Monster, Die* in the United States) that was based on Lovecraft's 'The Color Out of Space'. Karloff also starred, alongside Christopher Lee, in the 1968 film, *Curse of the Crimson Altar* that was based on 'The Dreams in the Witch House'. Lovecraft's name was left off the credits and Karloff died a short while later, as did the film.

The Dunwich Horror of 1970 was fairly loyal to Lovecraft's plot, but this movie, starring Dean Stockwell, Ed Begley and Sandra Dee failed miserably to capture the spirit of the Cthulhu Mythos or, indeed, the times that it somewhat embarrassingly

Lobby Card/Poster for *The Haunted Palace*, 1963.

Sandra Dee in a scene from *The Dunwich Horror*, 1970.

tried to encapsulate with lame psychedelic visual effects.

1986 saw the release of *From Beyond* helmed by Stuart Gordon who wanted to direct a series of Lovecraft movies, using the same cast and crew, in the way that Roger Corman had done with the stories of Edgar Allan Poe. He eventually managed to bring three more to the big screen – *Re-Animator* (from 'Herbert West – Reanimator'), *Castle Freak* (taken from 'The Outsider') and *Dagon*. He also made an episode for television's *Masters of Horror* series, *Dreams in the Witch House*.

Cult Movies, Sequels and Flops

Re-animator has become something of a cult movie, noted critic, Pauline Kael, declaring that she enjoyed the film's 'indigenous American junkiness'. Another well-known critic, Roger Ebert, wrote, 'I walked out somewhat surprised and reinvigorated (if not re-animated) by a movie that had the audience emitting taxi whistles and wild goat

cries.' It won a special prize at the Cannes Film Festival and spawned a series of comic books as well as two sequels, *Bride of Re-Animator* (1990) and *Beyond Re-Animator* (2003). Amazingly, a musical version opened on Broadway in 2011.

Gordon's *Dagon* of 2001 was a Spanish movie based on both *The Shadow Over Innsmouth* and 'Dagon'. It fared less well with critics and fans alike. Meanwhile, *Castle Freak* of 1995 did slightly better but was criticized for the brutal nature of the violence depicted.

'The Color Out of Space' was the source for David Keith's 1987 film, *The Curse*, which was for some unknown reason relocated from Arkham to Tellico Plains, Georgia. The 2000 book *Lurker in the Lobby: A Guide to the Cinema of H.P. Lovecraft* by Andrew Migliore and John Strysik said '[it] has it all ... everything except good dialogue, believable acting, and a cohesive plot.'

In 1992, *The Case of Charles Dexter Ward* again provided the background for *The Resurrected*, directed by Dan O'Bannon. O'Bannon was on familiar territory, having

Bruce Abbott has his head in his hands in a scene from *Re-Animator*, 1985.

written the script for *Alien*. Although it went almost directly to video, *The Resurrected* was described by *Lurker in the Lobby* as the best serious Lovecraftian screen adaptation to-date.

1993's *Necronomicon: Book of the Dead* tried to knit together three Lovecraft tales – 'The Rats in the Walls', 'Cool Air' and 'The Whisperer in Darkness'. Jeffrey Combs, who has appeared in eight Lovecraft adaptations, plays a character who finds a copy of the *Necronomicon* in a monastery and, locked in a cellar begins to read it. Perhaps this film should also have been locked in a cellar and forgotten about.

Renowned director, John Carpenter (*Halloween, Assault on Precinct* 13, *Escape From New York*) had a go at Lovecraft in 1995 with *In the Mouth of Madness*, starring Sam Neill, David Warner and Charlton Heston. The third in Carpenter's so-called *Apocalypse Trilogy*, after *The Thing* and *Prince of Darkness*, the film was a flop at the time but has gone on to achieve cult status.

A low-budget Australian movie, *Cthulhu*, based on 'The Thing on the Doorstep' and *The Shadow Over Innsmouth* did little to disturb the box office in 2000.

'The Call of Cthulhu', long believed to be unfilmable, made it onto celluloid in 2005 when the H.P. Lovecraft Historical Society distributed a silent film adaptation of Lovecraft's seminal story made by Sean Branney and Andrew Leman. It uses what

the filmmakers call Mythoscope, a blend of vintage and modern filming techniques that is supposed to create the look of a 1920s film.

The film was hailed as a great success, described in *Lurker in the Lobby* as 'a landmark adaptation that calls out to all Lovecraftian film fanatics – from its silent film form, its excellent cast, its direction, and its wonderful musical score ... this is Cthulhuian cinema that Howard would have loved.' Branney, Leman and the H.P. Lovecraft Historical Society were also behind the 2011 movie, 'The Whisperer in Darkness'. Again they went for a vintage look and again the film was showered in plaudits.

Cthulhu returned to the screen in an eponymous 2007 film, directed by Dan Gildark, based on *The Shadow Over Innsmouth*. The gay protagonist returns to his hometown where his father heads up a strange New Age cult. Although made on a tight budget, the film succeeds in evoking a creepy atmosphere.

Meanwhile, the least said about the 2009 horror comedy film, *The Last Lovecraft: Relic of Cthulhu*, the better. The last descendent of H.P. Lovecraft must guard a relic to protect the city of R'lyeh from rising and freeing Cthulhu. The Old Ones are played for laughs and there are even squid-like Deep Ones.

Of course, probably the most visible Lovecraft has ever been is in the character of Davy Jones in the blockbuster *Pirates of the Caribbean* franchise. Played by Bill

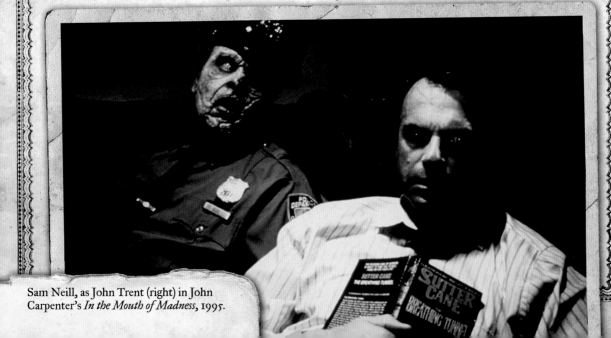

Sam Neill, as John Trent (right) in John Carpenter's *In the Mouth of Madness*, 1995.

Scene and movie poster for *From Beyond* (1986).

Nighy, the captain of the *Flying Dutchman's* cephalopod-like head and beard of tentacles is taken directly from H.P. Lovecraft's vision of Cthulhu – 'a monster of vaguely anthropoid outline, but with an octopus-like head whose face was a mass of feelers, a scaly, rubbery-looking body, prodigious claws on hind and fore feet ...'

Heavy Metal Lovecraft

Who knows what the quiet reserved Howard Phillips Lovecraft would make of today's music, especially that of the metal genre that seems to have a particular fascination with him and his universe? In 1998, for instance, American death metal band Nile borrowed from the Cthulhu Mythos for their album, *Amongst the Catacombs of Nephren-Ka*. Nephren-Ka being an Egyptian pharaoh whose cult was so unspeakable it has been wiped from history. At the end of the story, Lovecraft's narrator comes to a bad end. 'Now I ride with the mocking and friendly ghouls on the night-wind, and play by day amongst the catacombs of Nephren-Ka in the sealed and unknown valley of Hadoth by the Nile.'

Chart-topping American heavy metallers, Metallica, have delved into the Mythos a few times. Their 1984 album *Ride the Lightning* contains the atmospheric instrumental, *The Call of Ktulu* and their next album, *Master of Puppets* raids *The Shadow Over Innsmouth* for the song, *The Thing That Should Not Be*. The lyrics contain the lines: 'Fearless wretch/ Insanity/He watches/Lurking beneath the sea/Great Old One'.

American neoclassical darkwave duo, Nox Arcana, devoted an entire album to Lovecraft's work in 2004. *Necronomicon* features the ethereal atmosphere characteristic of neoclassical darkwave and song titles such as *The Nameless City*, *Yog-Sothoth* and *Dagon*. They re-visited the Mythos in their 2009 album, *Blackthorn Asylum*. Further metal Mythos leanings can be found on Californian stoner band, High

on Fire's 2005 release, *Blessed Black Wings* on which a couple of songs reference *At the Mountains of Madness* and in *The Chthonic Chronicles*, an album by English band Bal-Sagoth.

The music of Canadian rock band, The Darkest of Hillside Thickets is somewhat bizarrely made up of tongue-in-cheek homages to Lovecraft and the Cthulhu Mythos. The songs on their albums have titles such as *Goin' Down to Dunwich* and *The Innsmouth Look*. The band is named after a phrase in Lovecraft's story *The Tomb* – 'I will tell only of the lone tomb in the darkest of the hillside thickets' – album titles include *Cthulhu Strikes Back*, *Cthulhuriffomania* and *Great Old Ones*. In performance, they don costumes representing beings from the Mythos.

Finnish funeral doom metal merchants, Thergothon performed four Mythos-related songs on their 1992 album, *Stream From the Heavens*, including the fairly impenetrable *The Unknown Kadath in the Cold Waste*.

For something a little gentler, there was a band in the psychedelic sixties called H.P. Lovecraft whose haunting, eerie music was based on Lovecraft's writings. But, strangest of all musical connections with Lovecraft has to be the musical, *A Shoggoth on the Roof*, written by a member of the H.P. Lovecraft Historical Society. It was first performed in a Swedish translation at Miskatonicon, a Lovecraft convention in Sweden in 2005. Songs include *If I were a Deep One* (to the tune of *If I Were a Rich Man*) and *Byakhee Byakhee* (to the tune of *Matchmaker*)

Lovecraft on Television

David Warner once again appeared in a Lovecraftian work in 1991, this time the TV film, *Cast a Deadly Spell*. Fred Ward stars as Harry Philip Lovecraft, no less, a hard-boiled 1940s private detective who exists in a strange world in which monsters and bizarre beasts are abroad. Zombies are used as cheap labor and everyone, except

Lovecraft, uses magic. The film is not based on any one Lovecraft work, but contains many Lovecraftian elements and takes place against the backdrop of the Cthulhu Mythos. Throughout the film characters mention the *Necronomicon*, the Great Old Ones, Cthulhu and Yog-Sothoth. A 1994 sequel, *Witch Hunt*, followed with Dennis Hopper as H. Philip Lovecraft.

A 1985 episode of the *Twilight Zone* featured a Stephen King story that was heavily influenced by Lovecraft's 'The Thing on the Doorstep'. *Gramma* features monsters, the entrance to Hell and indecipherable books and Cthulhu appears in the 1987 animated television series, *The Real Ghostbusters*. A copy of the *Necronomicon* is stolen from New York Public Library by the Cult of Cthulhu. They summon him and he does what he does best by going on the rampage through Coney Island amusement park before being sent back to sleep.

In 2005, the *Masters of Horror* television series featured *H.P. Lovecraft's Dreams in the Witch House*, directed by Stuart Gordon who kept it fairly true to its source.

Cthulhu has also made several guest appearances in hugely popular cartoons. He turns up in no fewer than three episodes of *South Park* in one of which he is encouraged to go on the rampage and massacre Justin Bieber and his fans. In *The Simpsons* episode, *Cthulhu? Gesundheit*, Lovecraft's deity emerges from a tap and Springfield is overrun by monsters.

Lovecraft in Gaming

The Cthulhu Mythos, with its grotesque characters, hideous monsters and sophisticated history was tailor-made for today's gamer. There are countless role-playing and card and video games, of which there is only space for a few.

Investigate the deaths of the members of an entire expedition at the foot of a mountain range with the app *At the Mountains of Madness* or play the multi-award-winning

Call of Cthulhu. In its *Dark Corners of the Earth* version, a first-person action/horror game, as Detective Jack Walters, you can investigate Innsmouth as the heavens align. *Call of Cthulhu: Prisoners of Ice* sets you loose in *At the Mountains of Madness* territory.

If survival is your particular passion, then there is *Clockwork Empires*, described as a Lovecraftian sim where the objective is to prevent Imperial colonists from establishing a settlement on a new frontier where 'Other Creatures' live.

Darkness Within: In Pursuit of Loath Nolder takes place in the fictional Lovecraftian town of Wellsmoth where players are asked to solve the murder of Clark Field, a rich man who had been involved with the occult.

Meanwhile, other games ask us to try to keep evil at bay, such as *Elder Sign: Omens* and Clive Barker's *Jericho*. *The Case of Charles Dexter Ward* is adapted for the hidden object/adventure game, *Haunted Hotel 4*, set in an old hotel where the player tries to find Charles Dexter Ward who has vanished. The *Mass Effect* series of role-playing games is set against a Cthulhu Mythos backdrop, a similar location for *The Moaning Words*, which was devised by fantasy and science fiction author, Alan Dean Foster.

'A Genuine Cthulhu experience' is promised by 3D multiplayer online role-playing game, *Monria*, a chance to 'unearth the Church of Cthulhu's secrets'. Meanwhile, the first-person shooter game, *Quake*, contains many Lovecraftian elements.

The playable horror novel, *Robert D. Anderson and the Legend of Cthulhu* has both shooter and adventure elements. The protagonist, Anderson, explores a huge system of cages and caverns beneath the castle of his ancestors where the Order of the Black Sun practices dark rituals. The atmospheric *The Statement of Randolph Carter* is a 2D point and click adventure game based on Lovecraft's story and a dark, ancient force lurks in Red Creek Valley as private detective Paul Prospero tries to find a missing boy in *The Vanishing of Ethan Carter*.

H.P. Lovecraft's works have become major inspirations for computer video games' settings and storylines. (Above) *The Secret World* & (Opposite) *Alone in the Dark: Illumination.*

THE OLDEST
AND STRONGEST
EMOTION OF
MANKIND IS FEAR,
AND THE OLDEST
AND STRONGEST
KIND OF FEAR
IS FEAR OF THE
UNKNOWN.

H.P. LOVECRAFT

FURTHER READING

ABOUT H.P. LOVECRAFT

Harms, Daniel (2008) *The Cthulhu Mythos Encyclopedia: A Guide to H.P. Lovecraft's Universe.* Elder Signs Press, Lake Orion.

Houellebecq, Michel (2008) *H.P. Lovecraft: Against the World, Against Life.* Gollancz, London.

Joshi, S.T. & Schultz, D.E. (2001) *An H.P. Lovecraft Encyclopedia.* Hippocampus Press, New York.

Joshi, S.T. (2013) *I Am Providence: The Life and Times of H.P. Lovecraft, Volume 1.* Hippocampus Press, New York.

Joshi, S.T. (2013) *I Am Providence: The Life and Times of H.P. Lovecraft, Volume 2.* Hippocampus Press, New York.

LOVECRAFT'S STORIES

Lovecraft, H.P. (2012) *The Call of Cthulhu and Other Weird Stories.* Penguin Classics, London.

Lovecraft, H.P. (2004) *The Dreams in the Witch House: And Other Weird Stories.* Penguin Classics, London.

Lovecraft, H.P. (2001) *The Thing on the Doorstep and Other Weird Stories.* Penguin Classics, London.

CTHULHU MYTHOS STORIES BY OTHERS

Datlow, Ellen (ed.) (2014) *Lovecraft's Monsters.* Tachyon Publications, San Francisco.

Guran, Paula (ed.) (2011) *New Cthulhu: The Recent Weird.* Prime Books, Gaithersburg.

Lockhart, Ross E. (2012) *The Book of Cthulhu II.* Night Shade Books, San Francisco.

Lockhart, Ross E. (2011) *The Book of Cthulhu.* Night Shade Books, San Francisco.

Pirates of the Caribbean: At World's End (2007). Bill Nighy as Davy Jones, captain of *The Flying Dutchman*.

INDEX

Picture Credits

This edition published in 2015 by
Chartwell Books
an imprint of Book Sales
a division of Quarto Publishing Group USA Inc.
142 West 36th Street, 4th Floor
New York, New York 10018
USA

ISBN-13: 978-0-7858-3269-0

Printed in China